Community College Leadership

Community College Leadership

Strategies for Boards, Presidents and Administrators

GARY L. RHODES *and*
MARK A. CREERY, SR.

Forewords by Tim Kaine,
Dana B. Hamel *and* Edward Steiner

McFarland & Company, Inc., Publishers
Jefferson, North Carolina

ISBN (print) 978-1-4766-8252-5
ISBN (ebook) 978-1-4766-4364-9

LIBRARY OF CONGRESS AND BRITISH LIBRARY
CATALOGUING DATA ARE AVAILABLE

Library of Congress Control Number 2021044610

© 2021 Gary L. Rhodes and Mark A. Creery, Sr. All rights reserved

No part of this book may be reproduced or transmitted in any form or by any means, electronic or mechanical, including photocopying or recording, or by any information storage and retrieval system, without permission in writing from the publisher.

Front cover image © El Nariz/Shutterstock

Printed in the United States of America

McFarland & Company, Inc., Publishers
Box 611, Jefferson, North Carolina 28640
www.mcfarlandpub.com

Acknowledgments

This book is dedicated to the thousands of students who have attended community colleges and to the faculty and staff who have made the students' life-changing experiences possible.

We would like to thank our wives, Nam Rhodes and Amy Creery, for their patience in enabling us to take time away from our families for the endeavor of this book.

We would like to thank Rose Marie Owen and Susan Shibut for their careful reviews and edits as chapters evolved.

In addition, we would like to thank the hundreds of people who contributed to the book through their work as faculty and staff in a community colleges, as members of community college boards, and/or as thought leaders in the community, state, and nation who have collaborated with community colleges.

A special acknowledgment goes to the following individuals who personally gave their time and thought to this project:

Sherrie Brach Armstrong
Peter Blake
Benjamin Campbell
Hara Charlier
Elizabeth Creamer
James Cuthbertson
Glenn DuBois
Siobhan Dunnavant
Patrick Farrell
Richard Groover
Dana B. Hamel
Tim Kaine
Jeffrey J. Kraus
James Lane
David Loope
Whit Madère
John A. Manzari
John W. Martin
Sharon A. McDade
John J. Rainone
Theodore (Ted) Raspiller
Stewart D. Roberson
Kim Scheeler
Vaughn A. Sherman
Edward Steiner
Monty Sullivan
Eugene Trani
Belle S. Wheelan

Table of Contents

Acknowledgments — v

Forewords (by Tim Kaine, Dana B. Hamel and Edward Steiner) — 1

Preface — 5

A Guide to Reading — 7

1. Congratulations! Now What?
   Beginning as a Brand-New President — 9

   *Do's and Don't's from a President, Who Is a Woman,
   for Women* (Hara Charlier) — 14

   *Words of Wisdom from a Relatively New Community
   College President* (David Loope) — 15

2. Supporting the Cause or Leading the Charge?
   Dynamics of a College Board — 20

   Essentials for an Effective College Board
   (Vaughn A. Sherman) — 20

3. The Jenga Challenge of Higher Education:
   Aligning the Community College Mission
   and Strategies with Multiple Stakeholders — 28

4. Pastor or Symphony Conductor? The Nature
   of the Presidency — 34

   Building a Strong Executive Leadership Team
   (Sharon A. McDade) — 45

5. Who's in Charge? The College Board and the President — 51

Table of Contents

6. Pyramid or Funnel? Governance Structures   59

    Audits and Compliance ... "Tone at the Top"
    (Whit Madère)   71

7. Why Didn't You Read the Instructions?
The Need for a Complete College Board Policy Manual   78

8. Relationships, Relationships, Relationships:
Community Engagement and Leveraging Partnerships   91

    Business Community Involvement (Theodore Raspiller)   93

    Perspective of a Hospital CEO (Patrick Farrell)   94

    Perspective of a Chamber of Commerce CEO
    (Kim Scheeler)   95

    Perspective of a K–12 School Superintendent
    (Stewart D. Roberson)   98

    Perspective of a Four-Year University President
    (Michael Rao)   100

    Another Perspective of a Four-Year University President
    (John R. Broderick)   101

    Perspective of a Non-Profit CEO (Sherrie Brach Armstrong)   102

    Perspective of a Faith-Based Leader
    (The Rev. Benjamin Campbell)   103

9. A Beggar's Hand or a Vision? Fundraising
and the College   109

    Fundraising in a Small, Rural College (John J. Rainone)   117

10. Playing Poker with Wild Cards: Government Relations   120

11. Yin and Yang: Workforce and Economic Development   127

    Just-in-Time Teaching, Credentials, and Licenses
    (Mary Elizabeth Creamer)   132

    Workforce Development (Theodore Raspiller)   133

    Economic Development (Stephen Moret)   135

Table of Contents

12. An Achilles Heel or Seven Deadly Sins: Vulnerabilities That Can Put a College Presidency at Risk ... 136

  Lack of Political Savvy (Jeffrey J. Kraus) ... 138

  Seven Deadly Sins (John A. Manzari) ... 141

13. Walking the High Wire: Balancing Work and Play ... 143

  Role of the President's Spouse (Nam Rhodes) ... 146

14. A Solemn Duty: Hiring, Evaluating and Removing the President ... 148

15. Last Impressions: Leaving the Presidency ... 160

16. Sea Tides or Tsunamis? Emerging Threats ... 165

  How to Think About and Prepare Your Institution (and Yourself) for the Future (John W. Martin) ... 177

  Future Challenges from the Board Leadership Perspective (James Cuthbertson) ... 182

17. SYSK: Stuff You Should Know About Applying for a Presidency ... 188

  Faculty-Speak: Crossing Over to the Dark Side (Glenn DuBois) ... 191

  Strategic Vision of an Applicant for President (Sharon A. McDade) ... 202

18. Help at Your Fingertips: Key Organizational Resources ... 206

Appendix. Compendium of Presidential Search Committee Questions ... 215

About the Authors and Contributors ... 223

Index ... 227

Forewords

Tim Kaine
Member of the United States Senate

When I was mayor of Richmond, I saw J. Sargeant Reynolds Community College (colloquially known as simply Reynolds) as a partner in addressing many of the region's workforce needs. For example, in the early 2000s, a nursing shortage increased our local hospitals' demand for paramedics, who have the skills and expertise to alleviate overworked nurses of some of their duties. With a two-year paramedic training program, Reynolds trained and certified needed health workers faster than four-year schools could train new nurses; all the while, the school offered shorter-term certifications for EMTs to ensure our first-responder labor force was in good supply.

In addition to filling gaps in the labor market, Reynolds also helped workers build new strengths they could apply to their current jobs. As computers were rapidly changing the workplace in the late '90s, the school began teaching a half-day course called "Communicating Via E-mail in the Information Age." In that class, Richmonders and other Central Virginians could learn how to use email, acquiring skills that ranged from the basic, like forwarding and replying, to the more nuanced, like the etiquette of emoticons.

Around that same time, many workers in the region wanted to transition into more computer-based IT careers that required specific certifications. For them, Reynolds offered courses and guidance tailored to varying levels of incoming computer know-how. This variety of options helped students bridge the gap between their pre-existing skills and the skills they'd need to obtain the certifications for their new, more lucrative careers.

Those three functions—filling labor shortages, offering professional development, and enabling career moves—are just a few examples of the types of partnerships community colleges across the country forge with their cities and regions. They demonstrate how, as a population's needs change, a school must adapt to address those needs.

Community colleges serve an important function, for they open up the possibility of a bachelor's degree for students who otherwise might not obtain one. However, that function alone doesn't offer many options for students who don't want or need a four-year degree. The idea of what a public two-year college can offer students began to expand in the '50s and '60s to emphasize workforce training. In 1966, the Virginia General Assembly established a network of community colleges so that "Every citizen of the Commonwealth be given an opportunity to attend an institution of higher learning offering academic, occupational/technical, and community service programs at a nominal cost." Instead of just preparing for eventual transfer to a four-year institution, students at these 23 new community colleges could now obtain a two-year associate degree or professional certifications.

A half-century later, we are still seeing major changes in how students interact with community colleges. One of the most dramatic changes has been a move away from degrees as the near-universal end goal. According to the State Council of Higher Education for Virginia (SCHEV), while the number of associate degrees Virginia community colleges annually award has about doubled since the 1992–1993 academic year, the number of one- to two-year certificates they have awarded has more than quadrupled since that time, and the number of less-than-one-year certificates has more than quintupled! In fact, while these schools awarded slightly fewer associate degrees in the 2018–2019 year than they did in 2015–2016, they have steadily increased the number of short-term certifications they award each year in that same time period. Certificates now account for over 45 percent of awards by Virginia's community colleges, compared to just 25 percent in the early '90s.

Gary L. Rhodes and Mark A. Creery, Sr., know firsthand about the partnerships between colleges and their surrounding communities, and they have witnessed the changes I describe here. In the coming decades, the needs of students will continue to evolve, and community colleges will have to adapt accordingly. To prepare, we will need a new generation of community college leaders ready to guide their institutions through the upcoming shifts, challenges, and opportunities to serve their students. With this book, Rhodes and Creery will equip that next generation well.

* * *

Dana B. Hamel
Founding chancellor/chancellor emeritus of the Virginia Community College System

The lead author of this book, Dr. Gary Rhodes, has had an extensive and successful multi-state, 42-year career in community college education. His experience in meeting the challenges of a community college president has been outstanding. He has considered the challenges that face a successful president as "opportunities in work clothes," and in this book shares his extensive experience with the reader.

Recognizing that serving as the president of a community college is a high honor, Dr. Rhodes affirms that it is a unique leadership position for working in a community and offers many opportunities to serve the citizens of our great country.

The readers of this book will quickly recognize that this position requires a working knowledge of education, management, organization, finances, and of course, community relations. To assist readers seeking these positions, Dr. Rhodes has chosen content contributors who are recognized leaders in disciplines which are essential to the success of a community college, and they share their extensive and successful experiences.

This book is highly recommended! It is inspirational and a rich source of information for aspiring community college presidents, for members of community college boards, for deans, and others who are active in community college education.

* * *

Edward Steiner
Former community college board member at the local, state and national level

Mark Creery, the co-author of this book, has had an impressive career as an entrepreneur and business owner in the IT field. Creery has served on a variety of business and education boards. His involvement as a board member of a local community college in various roles, including multiple terms as the board chair, makes his contributions to this book particularly valuable. As an individual who is largely outside the academic universe, he brings unique perspectives to the function of community colleges.

During his tenure as a board member, the community college he served made significant advances that have positively impacted its students, local businesses, and the surrounding communities.

Preface

What Is the Focus of This Book and for Whom Is It Intended?

Our goal in writing this book was to help community college leaders better serve their students and fulfill their missions by providing useful and practical observations and guidance. Our hope is that community college leaders will benefit from our observations and recommendations in the pursuit of world class educational performance at their institutions.

We wrote this book for you: community college presidents, aspiring presidents, college trustees and foundation board members, executive and administrative staff, institutional advancement officers, and faculty and staff who are all part of the team that raises community awareness and makes a college successful. Whether you have been in a college leadership role for a decade, a month—or will be in one soon—we believe this book will prove to be helpful, useful, and maybe indispensable.

This book provides practical tools, insight into pragmatic strategies, and tactical tips for excellence in community college leadership. Its content is not based on university research studies, but on actual hands-on experience by people who have thrived in community college leadership roles.

Administrators of community colleges with leadership challenges may find value in this book as they work toward performance improvements. Ultimately, this book is about educating and arming community college leadership with the tools to transform their institutions into high-performing workforce and educational resources to the benefit of their students and communities.

Once appointed or elected, many community college presidents and board members feel their way through the job with a dearth of useful resources to assist them in their responsibilities. This book fills a critical need for today's community college leadership at a time when leaders face pressures on our institutions, including lack of state support, commercial competition, changing demographics, technological advances, and rapidly changing workforce needs. The authors' goal is to provide an untapped need for a practical guide on becoming the effective community college president or board member.

An experienced community college president and college board member, in combination with an impressive cast of collaborators, offer a broad overview over the rewards, pitfalls and possible solutions facing community college leadership. Throughout this book we indicate sections focusing on the presidents and college board members, or both. We believe the entire book will help community college leadership better understand the roles, responsibilities, and challenges for those who share the institution's governance and leadership responsibilities. We have attempted to capture relatable experiences that will be of significant benefit to you and your college—and, ultimately, your students.

Authors' Note to Our Readers

As this book was being completed, the COVID-19 crisis was emerging. We briefly address it in the chapter on emerging threats, "Sea Tides or Tsunamis?"

Certainly, the coronavirus will greatly impact how we teach and interact with our students and other stakeholders in ways we are just learning. We believe what we have written will be beneficial to community college leaders throughout this crisis and ones yet to come.

A Guide to Reading

Throughout the book, highlighted features will help identify key points and lessons.

- **Universal truth**—Maxims and principles to strengthen strategies, tactics, and behaviors.

- **Danger zone**—Cautions that, if ignored, can result in serious consequences for your institution and its leaders.

- **Anecdote**—Examples from the authors and collaborators that illustrate effective or harmful practices.

- **Helpful tip**—Practical nuggets to help college leadership improve the performance of the college and its leadership.

- **Key chapter takeaways**—At the end of each chapter there is a list of key chapter takeaways that highlight the most important concepts of the chapter.

Chapter 1

Congratulations! Now What?
Beginning as a Brand-New President

It has been said that it is more difficult to get a community college presidency than to be president. Although it's a stretch in concept, there is an element of truth worth contemplation. I was very fortunate to receive two offers for my first community college presidency on the very same day!

There is great pressure to land that first college presidency! After all, my wife and I had worked hard for several years to prepare my career and our family for the rigor, responsibility, and joys of finally leading a community college. We felt like we just couldn't wait!

My wife and I were returning from a cruise. We knew that we needed to return home quickly and pack for a trip to the upper Midwest, where I was a finalist for a community college presidency. Upon getting back to the mainland we discovered we were also invited for a presidential finalist interview in a northern state. We expeditiously made arrangements to attend that interview as well.

The first interview (the one in the Midwest) went great! The college board wined and dined my wife and me, and showed great enthusiasm for us as a couple. As I was meeting with the search committee, college board members, community leaders, and faculty/staff, others were showing my wife houses. She even found a house that we could move into and live in comfortably. We were all but ready to accept the job and begin the move.

However, at the end of the two-day interview process, one of the board members pulled me aside and said, "Dr. Rhodes, if we offer you the position of college president here, we will give you a few thousand dollars more than the president's salary, so that when the board goes out to dinner, you can buy the drinks!" This seemed odd and caught my attention. At best, it was an awkward thing to have said. I had to wonder about the college culture and how well ethics were both valued and managed. Despite the tempting prospect of my first presidency, I turned down the offer.

More Than One Right Way to Get Started: The Influential First Impression

It's important to recognize that starting off on the right foot can take many forms. A good start is fundamental to how successfully a new president or board member evolves in their role.

 Never forget that no matter how cliché it seems, there truly is only one opportunity for a first impression.

Develop Your "First Impression Plan"

Before you actually start your first day, there are several things you can do to make your first impression more dynamic and memorable. Although these are not all of the things you might consider, a good starting point is found in the list below:

- **Send a personal "thank you"** to those who helped you get hired or appointed. Times are changing regarding the protocol and format of such gestures. Still, a good handwritten note, a personal phone call, or a personal email will reinforce your care and appreciation. With that acknowledgment, the person with whom you're communicating will take pride in your accomplishments and can be counted on for future support.
- **Identify key stakeholders** (individuals and organizations) that interact with you and the college. It will serve as a priority list of those you should meet with as soon as possible, beginning with your first day as president. Ideally, this is a manageable list of a dozen or so stakeholders. You will want to keep this list handy, and review and update it from time to time.
- **Remember the power of personal visibility** and managing by walking around. For the most part, faculty, staff, and students like to see and interact with the college president. Most leaders recognize communications are fundamental to successful leadership, and one way to reinforce communications is to be as visible as possible in meaningful ways. The most powerful technique is "managing by walking around" and being visible in

1. Congratulations! Now What?

ways that seem to be natural, caring, and reinforcing positive values. Early on, demonstrable accessibility can pave the way for essential communications between you and your faculty and staff. Without disrupting classes, it's a good technique for getting to know faculty, staff, and students on a more personal level and can be very helpful in establishing the culture of the institution.

- **Research and study everything you can about the institution** including history, mission, vision, strategic plan, board bylaws and policies. It's highly important for new community college leaders to demonstrate that they understand and respect the history, purpose, and life of the college before their arrival. One way to jumpstart this is to study the school.

- **Ask yourself, "how new are you?"** Consideration should be given to the different dynamics for a president hired from within the college, moving up from a lower level position, versus a new president who was brought in from the outside. And although some new presidents may not be from their new college, they may have worked in the same state or community college system, and be known by some people. In any of these cases, there may be some issues with colleagues who were not selected as the new president.

An outside hire generally has the advantage of starting fresh with establishing their reputation and developing relationships with faculty and staff. A new president who worked in another position at their same college must be aware of the dynamics of having faculty and staff continue to think of them in their previous role. And in all likelihood, the president from the inside has developed relationships (both positive and negative) with different faculty and staff. In both cases the new president must clarify their values, lead with their ears, and clarify and reinforce their values and leadership principles constantly as they embark upon their new role.

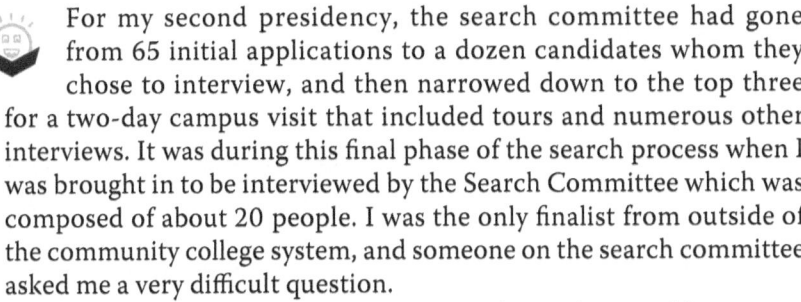

For my second presidency, the search committee had gone from 65 initial applications to a dozen candidates whom they chose to interview, and then narrowed down to the top three for a two-day campus visit that included tours and numerous other interviews. It was during this final phase of the search process when I was brought in to be interviewed by the Search Committee which was composed of about 20 people. I was the only finalist from outside of the community college system, and someone on the search committee asked me a very difficult question.

"If we were to hire you as our next president, what would you want to change immediately?" Being from out-of-state and not knowing any of the faculty, staff, or community leaders, and little about internal issues at the college, I replied honestly and directly.

"Being from outside of the college, I am not in a position to give you a profound response based on experience or data, but there is one thing that comes to mind. As you know, at my own expense I came to the city a day early and as part of my due diligence, I walked around each of the campuses. It caught my attention that near the plaza between the two largest buildings on the largest of the three campuses, there was a 2' high weed that, although unintended, sent the message that 'somebody doesn't care.'"

Since I was hired as their next president, I concluded that my response had not offended anyone too badly. However, after I started working at the college, I learned that one of the board members on the search committee was so upset that an outsider would make such an observation about his college, that within an hour of my interview he called the college president and the grass was mowed.

It can be very helpful to learn what people's first impressions of your institution are. Remember, there is only one first and generally, one last, impression!

Considerations for Day 1

Face-to-face meetings with key stakeholders

One successful strategy is to schedule 30-minute meetings (or at least a phone call) with the key stakeholders both inside and outside of the institution. This goes a long way to establish the initial relationship and send the message that they are important to you and the college, as you met with them on your very first day! Some of the stakeholders who should be considered include:

- College board chair and vice chair
- Foundation board chair and vice chair
- Faculty Senate president (could be union president in some states)
- Administrative Faculty Senate president (could be union president in some states)
- Classified Council president (could be union president in some states)
- Student Council/Student Senate leadership

1. Congratulations! Now What?

- Local chamber of commerce CEO
- Local economic/workforce development CEO
- Local industry council CEO
- President's executive assistant
- President's executive cabinet

Craft your elevator talking points

Before starting your first day, be prepared with several elevator talking points regarding your new role and future aspirations for the college that you will want to express to the many stakeholders.

Lead with your ears

Avoid drawing conclusions or making suggestions and listen, listen, listen to others to learn their likes and dislikes and points of view. A new president can learn a lot about their new institution by listening to everyone and reserving judgment until enough time passes to enable them to sort through the politics and/or personal agendas that might be discovered. Their first impression can be as useful as yours.

> **Nothing speaks as loud as your actions.**
> Common clichés of "Lead by example," or "Walk-the-walk and talk-the-talk" are good examples of cultural values that emphasize how important it is for the community college president (and the college board) to take action when needed, and to take appropriate action.

Ego Management and the Benefit of Monitoring Ego Growth

It's fitting as we discuss a new presidency, that we have an eye on avoiding a premature end to your presidency.

The slow growth of the presidential ego can be crippling. Over time this can harm relationships with colleagues, reducing the respect and authority awarded to the president. Power and authority are not natural born traits. Most college presidents have worked long and hard up through the ranks to earn the prestigious position at the top. Without care, the president can self-destruct.

Frank Casagrande, president of Casagrande Consulting, summed it up when he said: "College boards have the best presidents in the world until they don't.... It's a cliff!"

According to the American Council on Education, which focuses primarily on four-year colleges and universities, the average tenure of university presidents dropped from 8.5 years in 2006 to 7 years in 2011. A presidential failure does not need to rise to the level of the child sex abuse scandal at Penn State, the recruiting scandal at the University of Colorado, or the admissions scandal at the University of Illinois. It can be of a much lessor scale but with the same result.

In an interview with Glenn Dubois, chancellor of the Virginia Community College System, he characterized three categories of issues that can lead to an abrupt failure of a community college president.

Personal embarrassment—The president has done something so far out of bounds that there is no way the president can keep the job. E.g., there is a bench warrant out for the president failing to pay child support, or they got two DUIs in a period of only two weeks.

Guns blazing—With some presidents, in the first year they come on so strong and change things immediately, like major reorganizations or setting dozens and dozens of goals. The rank and file conclude that the president doesn't listen and isn't part of the team.

Rules do not apply to me—As U.S. President Richard Nixon famously said to David Frost, "…but when the President does it, that means it is not illegal." This problem usually develops over time. The president expects everyone else to follow the rules but doesn't themselves. They develop a sense of arrogance and invulnerability. They suffer from an exaggerated ego. Inevitably, when that arrogant leader gets into even a little trouble, no one will come to their rescue.

Do's and Don't's from a President, Who Is a Woman, for Women

Hara Charlier
President of Central Lakes Community College in Brainerd, Minnesota

- Don't be your worst enemy. Don't question your worth. Dismiss impostor syndrome.

1. Congratulations! Now What?

- Don't try to be what you think they want; be authentic.
- Do find an executive coach. We all have things we could get some help with.
- Pay attention to work-life balance. This is especially true (as a female) if you have significant home responsibilities. Take time for yourself and for things that are not work.
- Find a mentor (or two). They can help point out your challenges and strengths. Many times, these things will surprise you but is obvious to others (but they won't say). Mentors will be your biggest advocate.
- Given the opportunity, mentor others (pass it on).

Words of Wisdom from a Relatively New Community College President

DAVID LOOPE

President of Beaufort County Community College, Washington, North Carolina

The following insightful recommendations for what a brand-new community college president should do and not do reinforce some suggestions made earlier in this chapter:

Set the tone. From your first morning on the job you must recognize that every person you meet will be forming an opinion of you. Whether you like it or not, your ability to lead an institution is now under constant scrutiny. Even if you were already at the college in a different role prior to the presidency, you will be perceived—and rightfully so—in a different manner now. Be friendly and accessible, especially in the early days of your tenure. But, beware of staff and faculty who may have a hidden agenda or want to make an end-run around the "chain of command." Be confident but not arrogant; you're at a community college, an institution where admission is open access and the mission seeks to enable people from all backgrounds to improve their lives. Model the essence of the mission from day one: your "elevator speech" should focus on student success and the college's ability to enable such success through the work of faculty and staff.

Resist the temptation to focus mainly on your former area of expertise. A presidency requires you to focus strategically on both internal and external constituencies, and issues from a college-wide perspective. If you were a vice president or dean prior to your new role, it's likely you focused on a single area of administration, which may have required significant internal responsibilities (e.g., vice president of academic or student affairs) or external responsibilities (e.g., advancement), but not likely both in equal measures. Remember that you're no longer responsible for the day-to-day operations of the areas that report to you; that's the job of the vice presidents. Your job must now focus on the future well-being of the college as a whole, which means letting your old job go and working with internal constituents (faculty, staff, board of trustees, etc.) and external constituents (politicians, policy-makers, business leaders, system staff) to the extent that the specific issue requires. Be ready to think from both perspectives each day and to integrate those perspectives to arrive at the best decision on many issues.

Listen, listen, listen! Let's face it, you wouldn't be a president if you didn't like to talk and didn't believe others should listen to your ideas! That's okay to an extent, but remember that you may know very little about the college culture you're entering, especially if you were hired from the outside. Let other people do the talking in your early weeks and months so you can begin to understand the organizational culture. Likewise, folks both inside and outside the institution will appreciate the time you give them to share their ideas about the college, and you may just gain some important insights into the relative strengths and weaknesses of your college.

Identify a few key people you can trust who report to you. It may prove difficult in the early days of your tenure to know whom you can fully trust on confidential matters. Hopefully, your executive assistant will be one such individual. Very quickly, you will realize that a great many decisions—some large, some small—will percolate up to the president's office and require you to act. This will happen whether you want it to or not; it's part of the job, so get used to it. Many of these matters will require discretion on the part of staff in the president's office. You need an objective voice who can provide you with background and context for some decisions. Again, this could come in the form of your executive assistant, or perhaps from a sitting vice president, or even your human resources officer. Use the first few weeks to ascertain whom you can trust with your agenda and make it clear to this person that they must exercise discretion and confidentiality on all matters.

1. Congratulations! Now What?

Maintain a close and positive relationship with your board of trustees chair. Your life as a president will prove immeasurably easier if you maintain a healthy relationship with the board of trustees, which in many cases hire, evaluate, and, if need be, fire presidents. In fact, if you work in such an environment, the hard reality is that you serve at the pleasure of the board of trustees and only them. To this end, it is vitally important that you work closely from the first day with your board chair. They can serve as an indispensable ally to you in your relationships with other trustees and can usually help steer you away from potential pitfalls, especially in the political realm. In the first few weeks on the job, you may want to set up lunch meetings with the chair and each of the other trustees to discuss the workings of the college from their perspectives. Also, send a weekly or bi-monthly newsletter to the board of trustees to keep them updated on important meetings, decisions, and events. Start this from your first week on the job and make it a regular part of your work routine.

Send personalized thank you, get well, and condolence cards. Hand write these notes; you will be quite surprised at the number of people who will thank you for taking the time to recognize their gift, illness, or loss in a personal manner. Do not send such notes via email or text; that's tacky. Writing sends a personal message, which is especially important in an age when people are bombarded with electronic messaging of all kinds. Also, remember weddings are optional, but funerals are mandatory.

Remember the Golden Rule and practice it. "Do unto others as you would have done unto you." Many of us remember this biblical quote from childhood, and whether you're religious or not, it can serve as an important primer for your interactions with faculty, staff, and students. You can still make important decisions and lead a large institution without disparaging your colleagues and feeling the compulsion to remind everyone that you're "large and in charge," so to speak. You need to make your college a place where faculty and staff want to come to work each day, because they feel positive about the mission of the institution and appreciated for their roles in that mission. Get out and about your campus and take the time to thank your faculty and staff for their work; be lavish with praise, and make sure to let others know when a faculty or staff member has performed particularly well. These relatively small actions will build positive morale from the bottom up, and similarly build your reputation as an effective leader who genuinely cares about his/her employees. There is no substitute for this respect and goodwill. Truthfully, it's worth more than any trophy or plaque you'll ever receive.

Get to know policy-makers and politicians personally. For some of us, working with policy-makers and politicians is not an easy part of the presidency. But it's a vitally important part of your role as a community college president, because these individuals often control the budget for your college. It's very important that you make a positive impression with policy-makers and politicians through one-on-one contact. Reach out to them and invite them to campus for a tour or, if their time is tight, agree to visit with them at their offices. Provide them with no more than three items, issues, or matters where they can help the college, and make sure to inform them of two or three key areas where the college is making a difference in the lives of their constituents. Leave a one-page synopsis of your college's needs and accomplishments; these are busy people and they do not usually have the time nor inclination to read anything longer. Also, personal stories resonate with politicians. Be ready to tell them how your college has helped Joe or Jill in their district; this story may stick when your other rhetoric has faded.

Never, never take a public political stance, and do not talk openly about politics. This is good advice for everyone in today's workplace, where sensitivities are particularly acute. It is particularly good advice for new presidents, who are called upon to speak in public to large and small groups each and every day. Maintain a level of professional detachment at all times; everyone is watching you, whether you realize it or not. Remain apolitical at all times and make sure the college is not perceived as having a political agenda. You may have strong political views; keep them to yourself. You represent the college, which has to operate and thus obtain funding from state and local governments, no matter which party is in charge. Focus on the needs of the college and of your students, faculty, and staff, and play both sides of the aisle to this end without becoming partisan.

Be flexible, carve out reflective time, and enjoy the ride! Being a community college president is really one of the best jobs in the world! You never have to wake up in the morning and wonder why you do what you do, because every day you have the chance in a major capacity to improve the lives of your neighbors. To this end, each day will be crammed with meetings—some of which are unplanned—and fires that need dousing. Go with the flow, and enjoy the ability to make decisions with your colleagues that lead to direct, positive action. Be ready

1. Congratulations! Now What?

to prioritize events on your schedule, because there will be times when you are double-booked. As a standing rule, always take the time to meet or talk on the phone with a trustee, politician, or policy-maker, no matter what else is on your schedule. Likewise, make sure you carve out time in your schedule when you can concentrate on strategic thinking and items that require your focused attention. Most of all enjoy what you can accomplish for individual human beings each and every day!

 ## *Key Chapter Takeaways*

- Remember there only is one opportunity for a "first impression." Maximize that opportunity.
- Develop a clear list of key stakeholders and a plan to communicate with them.
- Be available—personal and frequent visibility of the president is paramount to success.
- Study, learn, and listen to everything you can about the institution.
- Carefully orchestrate the reality of and perception of the first day with a well thought out plan.

Chapter 2

Supporting the Cause or Leading the Charge?

Dynamics of a College Board

The Board's Role

The first chapter focused on addressing the roles and responsibilities of the college president. This chapter will explore the dynamics of a community college board (in some cases the board of trustees).

Experienced college board member Dr. John A. Manzari summed up the roles of the community college board in three critical areas:

- Ensuring academic quality
- Ensuring proper institutional fiscal responsibility
- Supporting and evaluating the president (hiring and firing)

How this harmony is accomplished across institutions may vary significantly. No matter the institution, a good dynamic between the college board and the president requires a clear understanding of roles, responsibilities, scope of authority, limitations, protocols, and more.

Essentials for an Effective College Board

Vaughn A. Sherman
Author, Essentials of Good Board/CEO Relations

Anchoring board behavior to key essential values can help assure effective governance, even when outside events create uncertainty.

2. Supporting the Cause or Leading the Charge?

1. Good board-president relations begin and end with **ethical behavior**.
2. The board and the president must **communicate** with each other openly, appropriately, and even-handily.
3. The board and the president must each know their **separate responsibilities**.
4. The board and the president should be **evaluated** annually.
5. The board and the president need to **encourage** and support each other.
6. The board must consistently employ an effective governance **process**.

Types of Boards

There are multiple ways a college board can be chartered, appointed, and operated:

- Some boards are elected; some are appointed
- Some boards have taxing authority
- Some have term limits for board members
- Some are primarily advisory in nature; some have full responsibility for the oversight of a college; and some are hybrids
- Some represent specific counties, towns, or districts; others are selected at-large
- Some have ex-officio member representation

Regardless of a board's origin and type, every board's fundamental purpose is essentially the same—to support the college mission of meeting the education and training needs of its service area students, and to do so by supporting the college president.

Why Serve?

Board members should be pure. Their motivations for serving on the board should be focused on helping the college, students, and community to the best of their ability.

Board members who took the position to pad their resume, take the next step on their career or political ladder, improve their community stature, "fix the college," or any of an endless number of ulterior motives, undermine the mission of the institution. **College board members should serve solely to support the college's efforts to educate and train their students.** This approach allows them to act in the best interests of the students without any conflict.

Just as a presidential candidate is asked "Why do you want to be president?" in a presidential search process, prospective college board members should ask themselves why they want the position, to ensure they are serving with the right purpose.

Board Responsibilities

Boards and their members likely have numerous responsibilities to support the college they serve. Some of these are implied duties and may involve nothing more than just showing up. This means practicing advocacy for the institution by being present at college functions, local official and legislator meetings, and other community and stakeholder gatherings. This also means regularly attending college board meetings, committee meetings, retreats, and other board events. A big part of the board member's job is representing the college and the board in support of the institution and the communities being served. Official board responsibilities are defined by state statute or state/local community policies.

> An important task for a college board is to undergo a careful survey of all of its official responsibilities. Then the board should develop written policies and procedures to ensure that complete and comprehensive processes are in place to address and manage each responsibility. It also establishes guardrails to ensure the board does not get involved beyond the scope of its responsibilities.

Designated college board responsibilities can often be found in state board policy manuals, state or local laws, organizational charters, and other official sources. Typical responsibilities, both internal and external to the college, can include:

Internal
- Presidential hiring, firing, and evaluation
- Approval of new academic programs and substantive changes in curriculum

- Approval of the discontinuance of academic programs
- Appointment of curriculum advisory boards and members
- Oversight of college finances and audits
- Budget oversight or approval
- Approval of investment policies
- Approval of facility capital expenses
- Advising on and approval of college planning, accreditation, and similar processes

External

- Serving as ambassadors and advocates for the college
- Supporting the college president with legislative advocacy, including meeting with national, state, and local officials
- Serving as connectors with local business and industry
- Serving as the eyes and ears of the community for the college leadership

Board Policies and Operations

It's likely that you will find a College Board Policy Manual in place upon your appointment or election to a community college board. This manual is fundamental to board members understanding their roles and responsibilities. It's a key tool to be used during orientation, and one that should be routinely used as a reference to remind board members of its content. That manual should include:

- Bylaws that dictate board processes and procedures for meetings, votes, and similar organizational needs
- Details on meeting and event schedules, internal college contacts, committee structure, and similar board logistics
- Policies that clearly spell out the source and scope of authority, purpose, limits, and responsible parties for every board responsibility

 If a policy manual for your board does not yet exist, a board project to write one should become a top priority and be started promptly. Details for a policy manual are covered later in this book. Another helpful source would be to ask a peer institution for a copy of its policy manual to use as a model.

Communications: College Board, President, Faculty and Staff

College board members have flexibility concerning how they communicate to the college president, faculty and staff via meetings, phone calls, electronic messaging (like email or texting), social media, or more.

Any board or board member communication with the president, faculty, and staff should be done with appropriate care. A college board member's call, text, or email can sound as if it reflects an official position of or directive from the full board. The college's faculty and staff may feel compelled to act upon an email from a board member contrary to established procedures. Generally, formal board communications to the president or faculty/staff should be identified through official board action or should come from the board chair, although in most instances the college board should communicate to faculty/staff through the college president.

A good rule of thumb is that outside of official board meetings, communications between the board and the college president should be through the board chair.

In one particular complicating instance, and despite this rule-of-thumb, one board member I worked with regularly communicated with email blasts that included the full board, the college president, the president's executive cabinet, and selected faculty and staff. Several times the board member was reminded why this was problematic.

Unable to stop the behavior, the board chair routinely "replied all" to the email blast, thanked the board member for his thoughts, and indicated it would be discussed at an upcoming board or committee meeting. This relieved the president (and everyone else) from responding to or acting on the misdirected (albeit often well-intended) communication.

Modern communications, like email, can be especially problematic. Email is fast and efficient, but presents its own set of problems. In text form, nuance and tone easily communicated over the phone or in person can be dulled and misunderstood. "Reply-all" may be necessary sometimes, but just as often it's annoying and can cause damage. In addition, emails may be subject to FOIA regulations.

2. Supporting the Cause or Leading the Charge?

That said, channeling all board communications to faculty or staff though the board chair is unnecessary and tedious. It is not being suggested that the board finance committee chair should never communicate directly to the chief financial officer about college board business, just that care should be taken in such interactions. While there are plenty of logical exceptions, board member communications directly to faculty and staff should generally copy the board chair and the college president. Content should be limited to matters germane to the board's scope of authority, responsibilities, and oversight.

Working Through a Board Crisis

Board members, whether appointed or elected, come from all backgrounds. Their motivations to serve can vary significantly. In an ideal situation, their motivations are genuine, and are something like:

- To serve in the best interest of the students
- To serve and represent their community and citizens in a fair and impartial manner
- To work with the college president (and the community college system when applicable) to advance the respective mission and strategic plan
- To serve as ambassadors on behalf of the college

Board positions are inherently political, so there can be complications. Perhaps a good friend of a board member wants you to intervene on behalf of a relative. Perhaps a program dear to your heart is being considered for discontinuation. Perhaps a board member requests car service from the college's security staff. As board chair, what do you do?

> One college had a former city mayor on its board. He was used to people listening to him. He enjoyed the spotlight. Often during board discussions, after most issues were talked-out, he would ceremoniously take the floor to recap the discussion using lofty rhetorical language to reinforce his eloquence, state his position, and lobby for his desired action.
>
> While he could be a bit tedious, his thoughtfulness and experience were useful to the board. As with all people, he deserved respect.
>
> On one occasion, a faculty member, who was also the former mayor's friend, needed board action taken on behalf of his department.

It was evident to everyone that this was not in the best interest of the students or the college. The former mayor lobbied hard for his friend's needs. As board chair, I saw the complication and tabled the issue. I then asked to meet with the board member for lunch.

At lunch, I asked to him to lay out his full position on the matter. I patiently listened. Afterwards, I echoed what I had heard and asked how he thought we should move forward. The former mayor knew his stated position was untenable. He simply wanted to appear loyal to a friend and capable of swaying the board's position even in retirement.

We agreed to leave the item tabled for the time being, where it died a quiet death. This prevented any embarrassment to the board member and allowed the college leadership to make the decision that was in the college's (and therefore students') best interest.

The key here was to listen to the needs of this esteemed board member, validate his worth and contributions, and allow him to contribute (and save face) as best he could.

As you might expect, the way forward in such a case is both simple and complicated. In the case described above, the errant board member took a position directly from a faculty or staff member. A big no-no! Had the board member dealt directly with the board chair instead, a little bit of counseling would have probably headed off any problems. But that didn't happen. The board member spoke directly to an instructor, or the dean, or the head of security, who likely presumed the board member spoke on behalf of the board, and felt they had no choice but to follow the board member's desires.

Because board members serve as elected or appointed officials, actual control over them is likely limited. That means resolution of such issues like these often requires great care. Specifically:

- Take quick decisive action; don't let issues fester;
- Arm yourself with clear policies or protocols from the community college system, college, or board policy manual;
- Find a way for everyone to save face whenever possible;
- Strive to reach an understanding with the problematic board member to resolve the situation appropriately.

When inappropriate board member behavior is to the extent that it can negatively affect the college, the college president may want to get involved. While this can be helpful, it can also make resolution tougher; so be careful. Board issues are the responsibility of the board (and the board chair). The president should get involved when the board chair asks and they both agree that the president's involvement is essential. Of course, if the problematic board member happens to be the board chair, the situation is much more complicated.

More serious board actions in the wake of bad behavior, such as censure or removal from the board, should be a last resort. Public pressure can create divisiveness that might permanently damage the board dynamics and, therefore, be harmful to the college.

Key Chapter Takeaways

- The role of the college board is to ensure that the institution fulfills its mission in serving its community and students through support of the president and the institution in a fair, lawful, and fiscally responsible manner.
- The college board fulfills its responsibilities via policy governance, oversight, advocacy, and strategic planning.
- Although the college board hires and fires the president, the faculty and staff are generally not the college board's responsibility and should not be treated as such.
- The college board's governance responsibilities typically center on some degree of oversight and review of academic program content, student life, financial, facilities, and operations.
- Remember that college board members serve to support the president and the success of the college.
- Study and learn as much about the college to effectively serve as an ambassador and bridge to the community.
- Recognize and respect the role of the college board chair as liaison between the college president and other college board members.

Chapter 3

The Jenga Challenge of Higher Education

Aligning the Community College Mission and Strategies with Multiple Stakeholders

Avoiding the Collapse

You've probably played the popular game Jenga. You start with a structurally strong, symmetrically designed tower and players remove pieces until it collapses. You win if you are not the player who removes the critical last piece, causing the collapse. Many of the pieces seem redundant, not core to the tower's structural integrity. The ones on the bottom (foundation) are clearly more impactful on the tower's survival. The ones at the top (the last editions) can be removed with little risk.

In your community college, your functions, charges, responsibilities, and initiatives are in many ways like the Jenga pieces except, if there is a collapse, everyone loses. Over time, resource constraints, new priorities, and changing times require some pieces be removed or swapped out for new priorities. The key is to understand which are the foundational pieces and which can be removed without compromising others or the organization itself.

Let's start with the foundation.

Why Are We Here?

Mission statements, vision statements, and value statements are often not appreciated. The obvious reason is that they are often crafted, approved, and put on a shelf. It is something that needs to be done, but what impact does it really have? How many employees know what those documents say? What impact do the words have in their interaction with each other and their stakeholders? When was the last planning meeting

3. The Jenga Challenge of Higher Education

interrupted by someone saying "Is that really our mission?" Despite the common lack of respect, these basic concepts form the *foundation* of your institution. They deserve your attention.

> To help ensure that the mission, vision, and values are not just put on a shelf, consider a monthly reinforcement program. Create posters highlighting these themes, place them in the halls, in meeting rooms, and in common areas. Begin each meeting with a reminder of the current month's theme.

It's not that difficult to be swayed from your mission; community colleges have many "bosses" who strive to meet the needs of...

- Their community as a vital player in secondary education
- The business community in economic development
- The relevant state and federal authorities
- Students, not only in education and skill development, but also financially, with transportation, and in other elements of their experience

Community college stakeholders represent a wide constituency, pulling and pushing you in many directions, making it difficult to stay in your lane. This can manifest in many ways:

- State and central/system office initiatives and mandates often seem misdirected to community colleges.
- Many local needs are evident (food, transportation, housing, finances); it's hard not to feel the need to help.
- Federal mandates, often far removed from the community needs, require attention and resources.
- Local and state officials exert influence for political goals.

With all of this (and more), it's easy to see how a discussion about a free breakfast kitchen, or affordable housing, or specialized workforce training, or four-year co-located classrooms, or day-cares, or any similar initiatives can drain your resources and distract you from your core competencies and mission.

That is not to say that these things should not be considered. That is up to you.

It simply means a community college would be served best if everyone clearly knows what the college mission and vision are. Then, at least, when being pulled in a different direction, everyone would know what is happening and why. Once you decide to address a new need, you can do so with a shared vision and disciplined planning.

Draft a Clear "Mission and Vision" Statement Anchored by Published Shared Values

This is most likely an off-site retreat activity. Ideally, this would be facilitated by a third party with relevant experience.

Announcing that you are drafting "Mission and Vision" statements may be met with some sighs and eye-rolling. Don't be dissuaded. That lack of enthusiasm exists because your team has been through this before in your organization and others, and it never really seemed that it mattered. Recognize and acknowledge that disconnect and make correcting this obstacle part of the process. Agree that the team will:

- Draft a meaningful "Mission and Vision" that reflects the needs of the community and other relevant stakeholders.
- Communicate and educate your staff, faculty, and stakeholders on your statement.
- Develop a mechanism for integrating behavior consistent with the "Mission and Vision" into strategic planning and practical day-to-day operations and institutional culture.
- Develop a process for regular review.

The Ritz-Carlton hotel chain trains their staff to behave with a set of 12 core service values. For instance: "I own and immediately resolve guest problems." Each staff member carries a wallet card with these 12 service values. These values support their mission, which says "the genuine care and comfort of our guests is our highest mission."

Daily, all staff members are expected to demonstrate at least one of these values and report how they employed it in service to their guests or other staff members.

Integrating your mission into the routine behavior of the organization will keep it relevant and help ensure your energies are focused on what is important.

Dedication to Quality Teaching and Learning

One of the key pieces of the metaphorical community college Jenga puzzle is ensuring that the students are receiving effective instruction and are, in fact, being properly prepared for their goals. Most community colleges have numerous quality initiatives to help ensure that what is done in the classroom meets or exceeds the needs of the students and the community, some of which might include:

- Faculty and staff professional development
- Faculty and staff evaluations
- Curriculum design and ongoing review/updating processes
- Student instructor evaluations
- Standardized tests for professional credentialing

Accreditation

Your initiatives are important and critical to ensuring that the college's core functions are being routinely monitored and improved upon. But none is more important than the periodic accreditation process. What sets this action apart is that the process is well vetted, involves thorough inspection of all of the relevant core college functions, is executed by an independent party, and involves future-oriented quality improvement components.

The accreditation process should be welcomed by your college and integrated into the behaviors and practices of the organization. That is, if you are *continuously* preparing for accreditation, positive results will be self-realized. The benefits will flow to your students and your community.

Dr. Belle S. Wheelan, President, Association of Colleges and Schools Commission on Colleges (SACSCOC) offers her thoughts on accreditation:

> Accreditation is a process that was started in the late 1800s by institutions to ensure that higher education was delivering the higher-level instruction of a college degree; and that it's worth pursuing. In the southern region, we had about nine institutions that got together and said "we need to make sure that we're all singing from the same song sheet and offering quality programs." It started with colleges that were teaching men to be ministers, and then women to be teachers, and then expanded from there.

Accreditation is designed to be an external arm that comes in periodically to help assure that the institution to doing what it says it's going to do ... and doing it well. Furthermore, it confirms that you'll be able to do it throughout the tenure of enrolled. It's all designed to make sure that the institution is strong and that everyone is doing their part, including faculty, staff, support services, leadership, and the college board. So, we invite peers who work at similar institutions to make sure that all is on the up-and-up.

New President

In most cases, when a community college welcomes a new president, it can expect some big changes. This is reflective of the president's background and experiences, the perceptions the new president has regarding the college's strengths and weaknesses, and the needs expressed by stakeholders when the president accepted the position. Typically, significant changes are needed and expected with a new CEO. In practice, most institutional behaviors, policies, and practices should always be subject to scrutiny and not simply accepting "We have always done it this way!" It might be helpful to ask...

- Should we keep doing this at all?
- Should we change how we are doing this?
- Should we be doing something different?

The existing senior management and the community college board can help with this process. Efforts should be made to counsel new CEOs on the rationale for existing practices, the cost of making changes or discontinuing, and the role that practices play in meeting the organization's mission. Doing this without sounding defensive is difficult, so a vetting methodology should include these considerations:

- Why are we doing this?
- Whom does it benefit?
- What would happen if we stopped?
- How could we stop?
- Is there an alternative or better way?
- What are some other ways to get the same result?
- Does this contribute to our mission?
- Is there someone else who can do this better or just as well?

This continuous improvement process could be well served by a scoring rubric, starting with the practices that have the greatest impact (largest number of students, most expensive, etc.).

3. The Jenga Challenge of Higher Education

 ### *Key Chapter Takeaways*

- Ensure that your mission, vision, and values are not collecting dust. Find a way to keep them top-of-mind with all staff members.
- Convene an offsite meeting (retreat) to develop or refine your mission, vision, and values, led by an expert facilitator.
- Your college is under constant strain to add more services or serve more people. Integrate a vetting process to ensure that any new initiative is in alignment with your mission.
- Changes in organizations should not have any sacred cows. Employ a rubric or similar tool to help ensure objectivity. An objective discussion considering a stop, start, or change to anything is reasonable.
- Embrace the accreditation process as an external mechanism to help you stay on course and foster continuous improvement.

Chapter 4

Pastor or Symphony Conductor?
The Nature of the Presidency

> "For some time, I have thought that the community college presidency is like a precious library manuscript. Presidents are honored by being able to enjoy the manuscript for a number of years and add their own chapters during their presidency, knowing all along to take great care of the manuscript as it must be turned in at some point for their successors to add their own chapters."
> Dr. Gary L. Rhodes, President Emeritus
> J. Sargeant Reynolds Community College

Role of the Community College President

The primary role of the community college president is to live day by day and hour by hour with the mantra "Is today's decision in the best interest of the students?"

That is the fundamental purpose of the presidency.

The president is the leader, the woman or man in charge, the boss, and the "face of the college." Although there are many leaders within any institution, the president is the most visible, generally has the most authority, and will get credit for many things (some in which the president had no involvement), and also will take blame on occasion (at times for something in which the president had little or no involvement). Ultimately, the buck stops with the president.

Early in my career, when my leadership roles were evolving and I was moving up in responsibility and title, I thought of my work as that of an air-traffic controller. I was required to keep projects, budgets, and people all moving in an intended direction, with my success being determined by avoiding metaphorical crashes or failures. However, it dawned on me one day that there was a major flaw in the metaphor of my work and career; air-traffic controllers don't typically enjoy the most beautiful

4. Pastor or Symphony Conductor?

part of flight, since they are not pilots or even passengers; they do not fly in the airplane.

The closest and most accurate metaphor for the community college presidency that I have since heard is that of a symphony conductor. Like the conductor, the college president gets up most days and determines what piece of music the orchestra will play. Like the conductor, the president determines the key that the music will be played in and sets the tempo. The conductor expects all of the musicians to play the same piece of music in the same key and at the same tempo. And above it all, the college president cannot force faculty and staff to play their instruments in the proper key and tempo; they must be inspired to do so. At times, all eyes are on the college president just as they are on a symphony conductor.

> Keep in mind that a symphony conductor, like a college president, is surrounded by master musicians who work together to create beautiful music, and all have a common goal and a strong understanding of music in their area of instrumental expertise. Their specific skills, however, vary widely, and range from percussion to horns to strings just as college staff have expertise in academics, financial aid, admissions, facilities, police, etc.

What many people don't consider, but is actually very much the norm, is that most conductors are familiar with multiple instruments and usually play some well. However, conductors are usually not master musicians themselves. Instead, they are surrounded by master musicians with the strings, the brass, percussion, and so on. The community college president is surrounded by master practitioners in academia, student affairs, financial aid, facilities, police and security, marketing, institutional research, etc. Like the symphony conductor, the president wakes up most days knowing that he/she will lead the orchestra, and that on some days the president will hand the baton to a vice president, maybe even take a seat as a musician in the orchestra, and play the fiddle.

The metaphor holds true; when college presidents conduct the master musicians of their institution well, the result is beautiful music serving the best interests of the students.

Leadership and the Community College President

If one were asked to summarize in a single sentence the primary responsibility of the community college president, one might respond:

"to provide leadership to faculty, staff, students, and the community at large." Ideally the response would include some element that describes the college president as empowering others' leadership as well. It is not the single woman or man wearing the presidential cloak who rules the world, maintains the good, and changes major things for the better. It is that proverbial "village" that the president leads.

Change is most often the result of many people exerting steady influence over extended periods of time. Human nature is such that it fights against change of any kind until reaching a tipping point. Then, change actually begins to take effect.

We could pick almost any point in the evolution of humankind and correctly state that those times were difficult; that the concept of leadership in that time was very confusing. In key local, state, and national leadership positions we find successful people whose personal styles and individual life experiences differ. Like snowflakes, no two people are the same. Yet, when we observe successful leaders, we find the common values of a community. But the interpretations of those values often diverge sharply, and sometimes even result in polar opposite actions. As children, our parents ingrained into us a sense of right and wrong and yet as adults, it seems much more difficult to make the distinction and act on it.

American democracy itself is being challenged in ways it has not been challenged in our lifetime. We seem to less often find common ground; instead it seems that the biggest bully at any point in time gets to rule the kingdom for the day. So, if our national leaders cannot successfully lead, how is a community college president going to do so?

Although it is rare that I use the word "always," I believe it would be correct to say that the community college president should always try to focus on acting in the best interest of the students.

The "Presidency" Is Grander Than the "President"

Often, I'm reminded that the "college presidency" is much larger than the individual who is president. This concept is very important and, at times, awkward to manage. People have expectations of the president that are higher than those of other positions at the institution. These expectations can be wide-ranging, from drinking habits to language to driving practices. It is important to remember that the college president

4. Pastor or Symphony Conductor?

can *never* take off the cloak of the position. The best chance at doing so is in the privacy of the president's home.

In terms of college operations, this perceived omnipresence seems to surface most often in casual conversation with staff throughout the institution, in which the president makes a simple observation about something on campus and the staff member takes that as a directive to go make something happen. And yes, I have learned that even when I prefaced an observation with "Please accept the fact that I'm not asking you to do anything or take action but only making an observation," many people don't "hear" the message because there is a fundamental need for staff to please the president. This is generally a good thing, but it can be disruptive at times if other college leaders perceive that the president is directing *their* staff or changing priorities.

> You will sense the dynamic of being "The President" on a regular basis in your presidency, and it is wise to never lose sight of the fact that the role is grander than you as a person. At times it will surface in almost humorous ways and its expression will vary, of course, from one person to another. In most cases, the staff member acts out of a desire to please the president, rather than out of fear of repercussions if they don't perform the task.

Living in the Presidential Fishbowl

Although senior staff like vice presidents, deans, and others are critically important to the success of a college, presidents may have felt at times that they were living in the proverbial fishbowl. The old adage "You ain't seen nothing yet!" comes to mind. It may take weeks or months for new presidents to meet everyone at their institutions and yet immediately everyone will know who the president is. You will feel at times that your life belongs to the institution. There are techniques to help alleviate the downsides of this aspect of the community college presidency (e.g., taking vacation time, spending time with family, a strong fitness/exercise routine) that can provide relief. You will, no doubt, need to adjust to the presidency. Remember, you volunteered for all this when you accepted the position. The ultimate reward will be great and beyond anything you could have imagined! You cannot avoid the fishbowl, so learn to manage it. Presidents' spouses/partners will be in the fishbowl as well, but nowhere to the extent that you will be.

Over or Under: Match the Speed of Grapevine Communications!

Shortly after dark, at the end of my first week of my first presidency, while working alone in my office, I heard someone just outside the door. Upon investigation, I met for the first time Arturo, who was the evening custodian responsible for many things, including maintenance of the unisex restroom in the hallway just outside the president's suite.

I invited Arturo to join me in my office so that I could hear his story and learn how he ended up working at the college and what his thoughts were about what we were doing well and what we might be doing better. I quickly learned a lot about a colleague who was passionate about the safety and cleanliness of our college campus, and who recognized that a safe and clean campus is a better place for people to work and for students to learn.

At the end of that conversation I was curious about something. The unisex restroom just outside of the president's suite had a commercial heavy-duty toilet paper holder (a two roller) that was designed so that no one could remove the rolls from the device. I noticed that one roll was positioned in the "paper over" position and the other roll in the "paper under" position. Attempting to be a bit playful and express my sense of humor, I asked Arturo, "Which was more correct in placing the rolls in the device?" and he had not thought about it. I replied that "It seems that in hotels they prefer the 'paper over' position rather than the 'paper under' position." After a brief chuckle, our pleasant "get-acquainted" conversation ended. Arturo went about his work, and I went home for the evening.

Immediately upon my arrival at my office the very next morning, I was told by my executive assistant that the college faculty and staff were abuzz. My conversation with maintenance worker Arturo the night before had spread like wildfire throughout all three campuses with the key message being "This new president is so particular that he is telling the custodial staff how to place the rolls of toilet paper on the holder!"

I wasn't sure whether this was a good thing or bad but I quickly learned how efficiently the grapevine worked at my new institution.... Warp speed!

4. Pastor or Symphony Conductor?

A Top Presidential Priority: Develop Clear and Strong Personal Values—and Promote Them

A primary role of the college president is to lead by example in word, action, and deed. It is imperative that the president have—and adhere to—a very clear set of personal values, recognizable by others. Every president will be tested over and over and over again, with the greatest frequency of testing, especially occurring when the president is still new in the position ("the honeymoon period").

Establishing these values will not only serve the college president well and act as a compass to guide the president during challenging situations when emotions may be high, politics cloud the situation, and/or it simply isn't clear what is "the right thing to do," but they also often end up guiding the institution as a whole.

A basic premise of leadership theory is that "managers do things right" and "leaders do the right thing." It must be remembered that inherent in the president's responsibility of managing complex operations, the primary role is to lead the college faculty and staff through good times, bad times, and the in-between times.

Chancellor Glenn DuBois of the Virginia Community College System would remind the college presidents from time-to-time, "It is easy to be college president during the good days. Presidents actually get paid for the few days a year when things don't seem so good!"

Clearly this statement was made tongue-in-cheek. It highlights a very critical point that presidential leadership is about sharing the moments of the good times with others, yet taking charge with clear values and a sense of purpose during the challenging times.

Shaping Institutional Culture at the College

As a parallel to clarifying personal values as college president, it is a critical responsibility of the president to shape and reinforce the culture and institutional values of the college. Every type of organization, whether it be a business, a non-profit, a church, or a college, has a collective institutional culture with values (clear or unclear). The culture is the sum of the organization's mission, values, and people. Although organizations change over time, the values that reinforce the institutional culture are relatively steadfast, or they change over a long period of time, as do social values. But during the tenure of a single college president it is most likely that impactful and clear values will remain constant.

The type of values that reinforce institutional culture are such things as...

- "Is today's decision in the best interest of the students?"
- "We don't care how much you know until we know how much you care!"
- "Anything worth doing is worth doing well!"

If we observe the most successful organizations, we see a pattern in which the values reinforce the organization's mission and ultimate goal of serving the customer or, in the case of community colleges, the students.

A New President's Values Must Be Affirmed!

On my second day as the brand new president at my college, I scheduled a comprehensive walking tour of each of the three campuses. Accompanying me on part of the tour was the vice president, who was responsible for overseeing college libraries. Upon entering the library at the largest campus, something caught my attention almost immediately. I observed that on the two dozen or so 48-inch round study tables throughout the library, every single table had in the center a red octagonal sign that read "No Talking! No Eating! No Drinking!" and I thought to myself that the first message a student would receive would be a strong in-their-face "No! No! No!" and "You are not welcomed here!"

Being a college president who was somewhat fanatical about reinforcing positive institutional culture, I said to the vice president something like "Don't you think that having a field of red stop signs as the first thing a student or guest sees sends a very negative message?" We continued the tour of the library and then the rest of the campus.

Fast forward two weeks later and I happened to be in the same library again for some reason and I noticed right away that the field of red stop signs was still there. I called the vice president and directed him to have all of the stop signs removed from the tables at all three campuses by the close of business that very day! Following up the next day, the signs were all gone.

It is often easy to become accustomed to the environment day-by-day, month-by-month, and even year-by-year, reaching a point when we no longer notice the details or experience our environment the same way we would if we were to enter for the very first time.

There is also something I call "culture creep" in which culture can

4. Pastor or Symphony Conductor?

evolve slowly sometimes in negative ways, and it builds upon itself—like particles of dust that you don't necessarily see as they are falling in the air but after a time the accumulated dust particles become visible and we realize it's time to dust the furniture.

The lesson here is to work consciously at seeing your surroundings with fresh eyes regularly, as if you were seeing them for the very first time. In doing so, you will naturally take steps to keep them clean, safe, and fresh and inviting for students, faculty and staff, and guests who visit on campus.

Relationship Builder: A Primary Role of the College President

A primary role of the community college president is to be the chief relationship builder. This is meant in the broadest interpretation of the phrase. Relationships must be developed, nurtured, and maintained with a wide range of people and organizations. Some of the relationships that are important to the college include faculty and staff (at all levels of college operations), student leadership, business and industry leaders, non-profit leadership, media (radio, TV, print, and social media) contacts, faith leaders, local elected officials ,state legislators and their aides, key state officials (including the governor, secretary of commerce and trade, secretary of education, secretary of finance, and the state workforce leader), students and parents, citizens of the college, and others throughout the entire college service area and beyond.

Presidential Rolling-Up-of-the-Sleeves

As a display of love and respect for the college president who preceded me and who successfully served for 26 years as president, the college foundation decided to celebrate him and his work by naming one of our major buildings after him. Plans were made and the event was scheduled with a large white tent in the quad that would easily accommodate around 200 people.

The afternoon before the event I invited my wife to join me for a personal brief tour of the recently renovated cafeteria. I was, of course, proud of the beautifully renovated space that would serve our students, faculty, and staff. Around 4:00 p.m., as I was completing the tour with my wife, I noticed our grounds crew hastily planting flowers to beautify our campus even further, knowing that more than 200 guests (including donors, local-elected officials, business leaders, etc.)

would arrive tomorrow for the event. I also noticed that a large field adjacent to the quad had grass that had not yet been mowed, and that we were short staffed, with the likelihood that my grounds colleagues would be working late into the wee hours of the morning if everything was to get done on time. I turned to my wife and asked her to come back to campus and pick me up shortly after sunset, as I was going to jump in and help our grounds crew mow the lawn.

I like machines. Having driven 18-wheelers twice, more than two dozen motorcycles over the years, and once an eight-row John Deere corn harvester, I asked our grounds crew chief to direct me to a 360-degree-turn lawn mower and give me brief operating instructions. Although it was quite hot and humid, I completed mowing the field a few hours later, just as the sun was beginning to set. Not thinking much about it, I walked around campus one final time thanking our grounds staff for their dedication and hard work, and wishing them well for the evening.

To my surprise, when I walked into my office the following morning my executive assistant informed me that there was an energetic buzz spreading throughout the college with the story of how the president had jumped in (literally with more than both feet) to work side-by-side with the grounds crew to cut the grass. I realized that had I spent upwards of $100,000 on something to raise staff morale, it still would not have had the same impact as the very natural act of helping my colleagues in a time of need. Needless to say, the event went very well and few people knew the story behind the scenes.

The lesson here is about caring and teamwork. People understand titles and the hierarchy of authority in the work environment, but they also know that underneath the title there exists a person who has the same fundamental needs that we all have. When the college president cares and can help others succeed in their work, everybody wins!

Internal vs. External President

Community colleges develop and mature over time. Presidential leadership needs to have different strengths and skill sets to best address a particular part of development of the college. Although many characteristics come into play, a common dichotomy is that of the internal versus external college president. The internal college president is one who focuses on and invests significant time with things internal to the

4. Pastor or Symphony Conductor?

college. The external president is one who invests time in community betterment by engaging community thought leaders and organizations away from campus. Regardless of which type a president is, it is imperative never to lose sight of the need to maintain a strong presence with the other. In other words, an internal president still needs to develop meaningful relationships with people and organizations outside of the college. An external president should never lose sight of the need that faculty, staff, and students have to engage regularly with the president on a personal level.

One example might be a president who, for health or other reasons, could not maintain the rigor and level of community engagement necessary to the office. Over time, this can result in a weakened relationship with the college's community and service area, and/or with the college no longer being represented at the table with other community thought leaders (business, government, non-profits, K–12 superintendents, and so on). In this example, the college may need a successor president who would spend time and energy on external relations and reinvigorate the college as a key community stakeholder in the well-being and continued development of the community it serves. And this would need to be accomplished without being perceived as abandoning faculty, staff, and students to develop those external relationships. Remember, "out of sight, out of mind!" has much validity.

Under different conditions and after the community engagement has been reestablished, it may be that the presidential leadership needs to turn its attention internally. They may need to gather the faculty/staff troops, refocus on the fundamental mission of the college, consider the specific needs of the community, and develop strategies and resources enabling the college to nimbly adjust to current and projected future needs for survival and continued success.

Balance is the key. There is no measurable formula that determines what proportion of external versus internal focus by the college president is needed. The determination should remain fluid. What is most important is that the college develop and maintain a reputation of being a critical stakeholder in community betterment, to the point that the leaders in the community instinctively want and invite the college president (and other college representatives) to be at the table when important topics are being discussed.

 A new college president must assess and not join organizations and boards too quickly. Fast forward, and when a president begins to get unsolicited invitations to join significant and impactful boards or meetings, that is a sign that development of external relationships is beginning to pay dividends.

The Art of Leveraging

Community colleges often are charged with doing more with less, and they usually have fewer resources (financial, staff, and otherwise) than their four-year counterparts. One way for a community college president to accomplish more and increase the impact of their college on the community is to learn to become a master at leveraging. Effective community college presidents learn to leverage relationships with other community leaders and with organizations. This includes the ability to imagine "win-wins" with other organizations that can benefit through sharing resources, and then being proactive in introducing such opportunities when the timing is right. There is really no limit to how community colleges might leverage their human and non-human assets to accomplish more.

Importance of Building a Strong and Diverse Executive Team

Among the most important responsibilities of the college president, along with clarifying institutional values, shaping college culture, and developing and nurturing a wide range of relationships inside and outside of the college, is that of building the strongest possible leadership team within the college.

With nearly 1,200 community college presidents throughout the country, it is natural that successful and unsuccessful community college presidents come in all shapes and sizes, different ages and ethnic backgrounds, and with different experiences. Just as people in leadership roles in business and industry, government, non-profits, and others are becoming more diverse, so is the college presidency.

Many successful college presidents would agree that much (if not most) of their success was the result of the strength of the leadership team that they developed and worked with during their tenure. It is important to attract—and continue to develop—team members with very different knowledge, skills, and strengths, yet who can all work together towards the common goal of serving the students though core values and effectively serve the college and community.

4. Pastor or Symphony Conductor?

Some years ago, as I was processing my life as a college president through metaphors, I was curious and wondered what the best baseball team of all-time was. So, I Googled it. A list of ten teams surfaced with the 1927 New York Yankees being listed as the all-time best team in baseball. The 1927 Yankees included Babe Ruth and Lou Gehrig, among other timeless icons.

At the next President's Executive Cabinet meeting, I shared my inquiry with my 12-person team and suggested that we look around the room. We had much diversity in age, gender, ethnic background, life experience, operational style, knowledge and skills, etc., yet we were a dynamic team. I told the cabinet, "We are very much like the 1927 New York Yankees. We have not won every game nor struck out every batter, but in the long-haul of the season, there was no team that could beat us!"

The point being: if we had been a team of all catchers, we would have had a dozen individuals who could squat by the hour and not be bothered by having a projectile thrown at a fast speed directly at their face, but we probably wouldn't have won many games. We would not have had the player who could run swiftly through the outfield to catch a fly ball or a player who could accurately throw a ball through an imaginary box with precise speed and curvature. The strength of my cabinet was the diversity in many things with a common goal achieved through clear values and teamwork, never losing sight of what was in the best interest of our students.

Building a Strong Executive Leadership Team

Sharon A. McDade

Practice Leader for Strategic Services & Senior Executive Leadership, Greenwood/Asher & Associates

A president—no matter how skilled and experienced—cannot single-handedly lead today's complex community colleges and universities. The members of the senior leadership team serve as an extension to and proxy of the president's leadership in each of the management areas of the institution. As a president is typically judged, for right or wrong, by the success of the entire team, it behooves a president to give substantial thought to the structure and composition of the executive team.

New presidents face two crucial questions regarding the executive leadership team. Is the team, and, by derivation, the organizational units of the institution, organized to best serve the needs of the institution now and in the foreseeable future? Are the right people sitting at the table? Many presidents can answer both questions with "yes," which enables them to move ahead at full steam. Many other seasoned presidents can recall the moment during their consideration of the presidency or the early months of their presidency when they had the realization that the answer to one or both of the questions was "no."

The structure question begs the most dramatic action. Organizational structures can capitalize on the strengths and interests of sitting members of the leadership team. For example, a chief financial and administrative officer may have accumulated a portfolio of responsibilities that are different from those assigned in a typical higher education organizational chart. If there are pressing financial issues, particularly relating to challenges of student enrollment, reorganization of the institution may need to be one of the new president's first actions. If financial issues are not pressing, there may be wisdom in taking time to analyze the organization and make changes slowly. The best scenario would be to convene a task force or to use a retreat of institution leaders to think collectively about the organizational design of the institution. Bringing in a consultant who can analyze organizational scenarios or a facilitator who can manage a retreat of senior leaders for focus on organizational design may be wise to ensure that the analysis process is transparent and includes all critical voices in the decision-making. These types of processes enable faculty and staff buy-in, and show that the new president will honor shared governance in decision-making.

Embedded in the decision of whether to reorganize lies a question: "Is this reorganization really needed?" Sometimes new presidents reorganize to make the new institution look more like the institution that she or he just left. If a particular organization worked at the previous institution, a new president might rationalize, then why not here? Alternatively, a new president may move things around to show action in the early weeks of the presidency. For example, the admissions office and the student success office can become footballs in reorganization design. Do these units belong into a grand design of student enrollment? Should they report to academic affairs? To student life? To finance and administration, because these offices are crucial to the financial bottom-line of the institution? Leaders of such units often tell tales of being moved around each time a new president enters the institution, with no apparent design to the moves or improvement after the move. Organizational design literature notes that it takes many years for a reorganized institution to reach peak efficiency, so it is essential always to weigh the short-term appearance of action against the long-term needed for full impact.

The question about the composition of the executive team requires other considerations. A new president would be profoundly lucky to begin with a senior team with superlative people in each role who are compatible with each other and the new president in every aspect. Since such instances are rare, usually changes need to be made. Additionally, some senior officers may be nearing retirement, and have held on to finish their tenure along with the president who just departed. Such leaders may choose to step out of their roles into retirement or back into the faculty as the previous president departs, leaving an opening for the new president to fill immediately. Other senior officers may choose to depart after the new president has completed the first year, so that there is overlap and continuation. Sometimes, one or more of the senior officers may have competed for the presidency, which may create an uneasy situation that needs to be sorted out. Other senior leaders will see the advent of a new president as a signal or opportunity to strike out in search of presidencies at other institutions.

Business literature and some leadership literature advocates quick action if a president ascertains that the people sitting around the cabinet table are not the ones with which to go the distance. This "rip-the-Band-Aid-off-quickly" school of thought calls for resignations of all cabinet members on the first day of the new president's tenure to give the new president the opportunity to sort out who should remain. The thinking is that it is better to make a move and get new people in place quickly so the new president and executive team can move forward expediently to address the pressing issues of the institution. If a president is hired by the board of trustees as an agent of change to take immediate action to save the institution with an understanding in the hiring process that a new executive team is needed, then the board can help communicate the critical nature of such change to mitigate its pain. Many downsides emanate from quick action. There will be a deep-seated distrust of the president that will linger and undermine their ability to get things accomplished over the long term. New hires may not ever completely trust the president not to make similar purges in the future.

It is difficult to run several simultaneous searches for new senior hires, with searches complicated by a prospects' concern as to why so many positions are open at the same time. The quality of applicants may be diminished because of concerns about the turnover of so many senior officers. These negatives suggest that unless there is exigency that necessitates radical replacement and reconfiguration of the senior team, there may be far more benefits to taking time to work through the replacement process to get the desired team in place.

In today's environment, a president communicates essential values about diversity through the composition of the executive team. While there may be little diversity in an inherited executive team, today's institutional communities expect that the president will attempt to diversify the team with each new hire. There is now extensive research in the business world about how a genuinely diversified board and leadership team will ensure more effective decision-making that takes into consideration a broader range of data and brings to bear a greater depth of knowledge. A diverse executive team reduces the risks of groupthink and increases team understanding of the institution's mission and its key consumers—students.

Diversity is most often defined as relating to those characteristics enumerated in an institution's official inclusiveness statement. For an executive team, diversity also needs to include areas of expertise, networks, and leadership orientations as well as the diversity of educational pathways and disciplinary expertise. During the hiring process, these types of diversity are not as often taken into consideration compared to years of experience and types of expertise. While it takes time and effort to build a high performing team from leaders with multiple layers of diversity, research is unequivocal that the long-term benefits make the effort worthwhile.

Four Scenarios for Any Meeting

As president, you will call and lead many meetings. Your meeting style will go a long way to ensuring that these meetings are effective and achieve their goals.

Of course, there are the basics:

- Starting and ending on time
- Inviting only those who need to participate

4. Pastor or Symphony Conductor?

- Having a fully developed agenda, with a clear meeting purpose and goals
- Ensuring the meeting sticks to the agenda
- Recording notes to capture thoughts, decisions, and next actions

But there is more. The two fundamental opportunities of any meeting are:

1. The opportunity to give or contribute something helpful to the purpose of the meeting; and
2. The opportunity to take something valuable away from the meeting—something that is valuable to the organization or to the meeting participants.

Based on these, it can be helpful to understand that there are four possible scenarios for any meeting. This is true whether it be a phone call, a face-to-face meeting, a Zoom meeting, or any other form of meeting. Of the four possible scenarios, one is great, two are good, and the fourth is deadly. The table below illustrates the concept of the four scenarios.

	Meaningful Takeaway & Opportunity to Give	**Opportunity to Give**	
GREAT!	Participants learn something AND have an opportunity to give.	Participants have an opportunity to give something to the meeting that adds value to the discussion.	**GOOD**
	Meaningful Takeaway	**No Meaningful Takeaway & No Opportunity to Give**	
GOOD	Participants learn something that is meaningful to them and/or to their organization.	People will stop attending if this occurs very often.	**DEADLY**

Before a meeting starts, the organizer should be able to identify possible opportunities for both contributing and taking something meaningful away from the meeting. One might even take the position that if these are not identified before a meeting is even scheduled, that it is premature for a meeting to take place.

In Conclusion...

The community college presidency is very special and unique position in that the "presidency" is bigger than the person who is president. A successful presidency requires clear and strong personal values that can help shape the institutional values. Successful community college presidents come with different backgrounds and leadership styles and there is no single "right" way to be a successful community college president. Ultimately, it is about leadership and inspiration, establishing and reinforcing clear values. The individual needs to craft their own magical combination of knowledge, skills, and strengths to meet the needs of their institution during the time they serve as president.

Key Chapter Takeaways

- The "presidency" is much bigger than the person who is president.
- The college president *always* lives in a fishbowl, and you must learn to manage it.
- Have clear and strong personal values and try to consistently live by and reinforce them.
- Through collaboration, develop clear and strong institutional values.
- Recognize "reality" and the "perception of reality" and when to focus on either or both.
- Creating a strong, loyal, and diverse executive team will be imperative to the president's success.

Chapter 5

Who's in Charge?
The College Board and the President

Boundaries and Limits

The president would be well served to understand that they do not run the board. The board, through its board chair, manages itself within its policies.

Likewise, board members would be well served to understand that they do not run the college. The president and the college's administrators and faculty and staff do so, via policies and limits established by the board, the system office, and other regulating institutions.

That being said, the college board and college president have shared responsibility for each other's success, and they play instrumental roles in shared governance. This can be done well only if boundaries and limits are well understood.

To the Board Member: How Would You Handle These Situations?

- The windows outside of the library have a disturbing film of grime from years of neglect—one of those things that you might not notice if you were around every day. As a college board member, you are accompanying a guest with a walking tour of the campus and he politely comments that it might be time to wash the windows. The guest is your county supervisor, responsible for your appointment and local funding for the college. You are momentarily embarrassed but recover quickly and say "Wow, I walk by the building all the time, and just never noticed it. That's the beauty of a fresh set of eyes. Thank you. I will speak to someone about this right away." You know well that campus upkeep and aesthetics play a large role in college choice and satisfaction. If the windows are neglected, what else is not getting the attention needed?

Do you:

- Grab a ladder and a squeegee and get to washing?
- Call the president and relate the encounter?
- Call Joe in maintenance and ask him to take care of it?

Admittedly, that was an easy one. While Joe is the obvious point man on this, a call or note to the president relaying the conversation is the clear choice. If the roles and responsibilities of the president, board members, faculty and staff are clear and respected, the windows will soon get the attention they need *through the appropriate channels*.

- In another scenario, your mother-in-law calls you. Cassie, her 19-year-old granddaughter—your niece—has a problem with her grade in Psych 101. Your mother-in-law is no dummy; she went straight to you because of your position on the college board. Apparently, Cassie was attending the funeral of a young friend and missed the exam. According to your mother-in-law, prior to the exam, she emailed the instructor to explain the situation and ask for a reschedule. Your well-intentioned mother-in-law sent you a copy of the email. Once Cassie resurfaced, the instructor said he was never contacted, did not see any email, and it was past the deadline to make up the exam. You know the instructor, a seasoned professional with whom you have had several pleasant and professional conversations.

Do you:

- Stop by his office and ask what happened? Surely this is a misunderstanding.
- Call the president and ask him to look into it?
- Call Cassie and suggest she schedule a meeting with a student advisor or program head?

This is tougher. A small professional courtesy from the instructor would go a long away to keeping the peace at home and with the family. A call to the president puts him/her in a very tough spot. If the president intervenes, the instructor would likely (and correctly) feel as if the president is way out of bounds on the management of his classroom and students. If the president doesn't, there is a risk of spoiling a critical president-board member relationship. Your relationship with the

5. Who's in Charge?

president would never quite be the same. The student advisor is the way to go, but unlike your mother-in-law, you need to remove yourself from any involvement. The weight of the presidency and board should not be part of any resolution here.

Tricky, problematic scenarios like these can occur frequently in most organizations, and definitely at community colleges. Knowing what to do can be difficult and very thought-provoking. Sometimes even the "experts" can disagree on the "right" answer. It is not enough to count on an encyclopedia of similar scenarios that fit the problem *du jour*. Instead, you are better served by a well thought out strategy and process for responsibility and control within your organization.

 Unclear or shared responsibilities and authority are rarely helpful and usually harmful.

We might suggest you start by defining clear roles within your organization; specifically, the president, the board, the board's chair, the president's cabinet, and anyone else that might feel they should have a say in college matters. The stakeholders have to agree to these roles and the protocols that follow, providing consistency, fairness, and clarity, with a focus on serving the best interests of the students.

 A general rule is that when dealing with college matters, the president is responsible for communicating and interacting with internal stakeholders, including the faculty, staff, students, and system office.

Jointly, board members and the president share responsibilities in communicating with and interacting with the elected officials, service area citizens, business leaders, donors, and others.

In this chapter, we will begin at the beginning by giving you a clearer picture of the proper roles of the president and the college board. With about 1,200 community colleges in our nation, each with their own president or CEO, and over 6,500 trustees, this seems like a good place to start.

A "Special" Relationship: The College President and the Board Chair

College boards come in all sizes, from a handful to more than a dozen members. Their influence and responsibilities vary from advisory to governance to hybrids. How they were selected, appointed, or elected can matter. And, of course, the varied backgrounds, experiences, expectations, and points of view matter. These dynamics in many ways create the "special sauce" of the board and help it fulfill its mission for the community college, the students, and the community. However, broadly diverse points of view, interests, agendas, causes, and concerns can be impossible to manage and support if left unchecked. Thus, the role of the board chair is critical to ensuring that the board has a collective voice, imperative to the successful conduct of its business.

In "Boards That Make a Difference" 2006, John Carver, renowned expert on board operations and policy governance states:

> It is the board's responsibility to govern; the board has a commensurate authority to govern. Individual board members do not. That is, whatever authority is legitimately wielded by a board is wielded by the board as a group. **Hence, a CEO is bound by what the board says, but never by what any board member says.** A board should pledge to its CEO that it will never hold him or her accountable for keeping board members happy as individuals and will never hold him or her accountable for any criteria except those expressed officially by the full board. In other words, the board as a body is obligated to protect its staff from the board as individuals.

That collective voice is embodied in the board chair. That is, the chair speaks for the board. The role of the chair is unlike that of other board members, in that the chair's communication to the college president represents the college board's position. In many cases this is done by board action, but sometimes it is done person-to-person. As such, great care should be taken by the board chair to ensure that what he/she says to the president reflects the board's collective position. Likewise, the other board members should recognize this protocol and tread lightly.

Finally, it can be helpful for the board chair to be briefed on emerging issues or sensitive matters within the college that might warrant future board attention to avoid such problems catching the board off-guard. The board chair can then determine when and if the full board needs to be involved and how.

Dynamics with the Full College Board

Ideally, the makeup of the college board will factor in the needs of the college and the community, and will comprise a diverse group from different professional, socio-economic, cultural demographic backgrounds. Board members should be dedicated to the success of the college's students by supporting the college and college system's mission.

Some boards are appointed and some are elected. They can range in size and are subject to different term limits. Community college boards are generally intended to reflect their constituents; they represent the collective voice of their communities within the college service area. Thus, there are many variations of boards. and every board is unique in some way.

The college president and the college board have a special relationship, in large part because the board uniquely supports the president in a number of ways:

- The president counts on the board to be critical eyes and ears in the community to ensure that the community's needs are being met.
- The president counts on the board to be a sounding board for policy, service, and curriculum changes across many college stakeholders.
- The president counts on the board members to advocate within their sphere of influence on behalf of college initiatives and needs.
- The president counts on the board to support his or her role with meaningful performance evaluations and coaching to support the mission of the college and professional growth.

The president does not expect the board to run the college nor, for that matter, dictate how it will be run. Rather, the president expects the board to adopt clear policies with appropriate limits (guardrails) consistent with its scope of authority, system policies, and the college mission. This helps ensure that:

- The president understands what the board values in the running of the institution.
- The president knows when the board needs to be made aware of situations that might threaten to strain policy limits or complicate something important to the college *or the community*.
- The president is well equipped to know when board involvement is necessary in emerging situations that might require support, advocacy, and/or other board actions.

Therefore, the president's relationship with the board should be carefully limited to these prescribed needs and responsibilities. Care should be taken by the president and the board to ensure that involvement outside of these parameters is avoided. Ignoring this caution can result in the board's quickly reaching a point of expecting updates on day-to-day operations of the college and feeling empowered to weigh in on them.

As long as the college is operating within approved board and system policies, the board should not have involvement in the management of faculty and staff, the handling of any individual student's needs, expenditures, or operations, unless explicitly directed as a board responsibility. Still, the president needs well calibrated antenna to understand when an issue that may not be specifically addressed in policy warrants board involvement.

When the president communicates with the board, it's usually in the framework of three main categories.

- The board should be informed or briefed about some matters (e.g., a criminal incident on campus, the inclement weather policy, a list of degree programs).
- The college needs official board action (e.g., approval for a capital project, a degree program is being discontinued, tuition is being increased).
- The college needs board involvement or advocacy among stakeholders (e.g., considering closing a campus, a need for additional local or state funding).

Finally, with limited exception, interactions between the board and the president should be at the full board level or with the chair, not with the individual board member. **The board should act and speak as one** and the president should communicate accordingly. That does not preclude a president and board member from sharing a meal. But, just as the board member should not be speaking on behalf of the board unless directed to do so by board action, the president should not be communicating to a portion of the board, excluding others. Exceptions to this were discussed earlier in this chapter regarding the special role of the college board chair.

The President's Role in Board Member Development

We will spend some time later in this book discussing how best to orient a new board member. Still, this is a good place to mention that the president can play an instrumental part of any board member's orientation, development, and familiarity with the institution. That could range from tours of the campus facilities, introduction to key staff and faculty, and review of college strategic planning and initiatives, overview of the budget, and more. This can be further accomplished with:

- Periodic reports to the board from various college functions by the responsible staff;
- Board member invitation to planning processes, especially periodic strategic planning events;
- In-depth briefings by senior college management at retreats;
- Invitations to college events such as symposiums, book readings, art shows, and the lie.

Evaluating the President

Board responsibilities regarding presidential performance evaluations vary greatly. In some cases, there is no local board involvement; in others, the board has full responsibility for this function. Regardless of the job, a regularly scheduled, well defined, and systematic performance evaluation consisting of qualitative and quantitative measures can play a critical role in ensuring performance and job satisfaction.

Hiring and Removing the President

Some community college boards have full authority and control over the selection, hiring, and removal of a president. Some have limited roles. Some have none. Regardless of these duties and responsibilities, the hiring and firing of the chief executive is likely the most important role of any college board. The action requires clear delineation of responsibility and process, consistency, and the recognition that these efforts are public, inherently political, and affect the college, the individuals, and ultimately, the students.

With regard to these duties, the board's first responsibility is to have a clear and undisputed understanding of its role, responsibility, and limits. Secondly, defining and documenting a clear and fair process is required. This process should be vetted against human resource policy, legal considerations, and other regulations and requirements.

The last thing college board members want is to find themselves considering hiring or firing a president without a formal, vetted policy to guide them.

In Chapter 14, we will take a deeper dive into the critical board responsibilities of evaluating, hiring, or removing a president.

 ## *Key Chapter Takeaways*

- Pay close attention to the board's role; avoid getting involved in day-to-day operations, activities, or problem solving.
- A general rule is that when dealing with college matters, the president is responsible for communicating and interacting with internal stakeholders, including the faculty, staff, students, and system office.
- While the board "speaks with one voice," the college board chair and the college president enjoy a special relationship that includes counseling each other to help most effectively manage the institution and fulfill its mission.
- Many college boards have responsibilities regarding the hiring, evaluation, and removal of the president. Be cognizant of this responsibility so that this duty can be handled in a thorough, fair, and professional manner.

Chapter 6

Pyramid or Funnel?
Governance Structures

Everyone Has a Boss

We all report to someone. Whether the CEO or the janitor, we all have bosses—probably several people or organizations. Most organizations consider their key clients, customers, or users their primary responsibilities; aka the bosses.

Our multiple bosses can often be demanding and pull us in different directions. Beyond them are other stakeholders who can demand a lot of energy and attention. In fact, the more senior the position you hold, the more likely that your list of "bosses" is larger.

These bosses dictate where you and your community college spend a lot of resources. They influence your decisions and may set many of your priorities. The need to satisfy a large group of stakeholders demands clarity, discipline, transparency, and precision in your organization's governance practices.

The Serenity Prayer

Regardless of your spiritual beliefs, the Serenity Prayer has proven to be comforting and practical to many: "May God grant me the serenity to accept the things I cannot change; courage to change those things I can; and the wisdom to know the difference."

Complex organizations, especially public-sector ones, are replete with rules, limitations, policies, and procedures that can seem onerous, byzantine, and irrational. You could wallow in anger or frustration or you could deal with it.

 Under difficult circumstances, sometimes the best you can do is accept the situation and find a way to optimize your institution in light of the constraints.

For instance, in some community college systems, the colleges are ranked based on their facilities' efficiency (how full the classrooms are). Then, those that are highly ranked (very efficient, usually the larger colleges) pay a subsidy to support those that are ranked lower. The intent is to provide financial support to rural, small community colleges where local access is more important than demand demographics and operational efficiencies. However, the policy has the unintended consequence of disincentivizing college efficiency.

Frustrating? Yes! However, it is baked into the system—so make the best of it.

An effective college president and board recognize what is beyond their control, learn the practical limits of their discretion/authority, and work toward the best outcomes on behalf of the students and other constituents. Time on the job will help you understand if there are gaps between perceived limits and actual limits. Your peers can help you navigate the system to allow your college to be the best it can be under the circumstances.

Governance Structures

Several states have a statewide community college system with individual colleges varying widely in structural organization, autonomy, and relationship to the system.

Community colleges in South Carolina and North Carolina have local boards with most non-tuition funding coming from local taxes. The funds do not go through a central office, and colleges function as a loose federation. In South Carolina, for example, the system president of the South Carolina Technical College System does not hire and fire presidents. That responsibility rests fully with the local college boards. The system president has more of a coordinating role with the 16 technical and community colleges and serves as a statewide advocate with the state legislature.

Virginia, on the other hand, has a more tightly knit statewide system with 23 community colleges (40 campuses around the state) and all college presidents reporting directly to the chancellor of the Virginia Community College System (VCCS).

There are two levels of oversight boards for community colleges in Virginia. The first, the State Board for Community College, has a board with members appointed by the governor of the Commonwealth of

6. Pyramid or Funnel?

Virginia. The State Board hires and fires the chancellor (and technically approves the hiring and firing recommendations of the chancellor for community college presidents). The State Board supports the chancellor in advocating with the state legislature.

In addition to the state board, each college has a local board that is appointed by local officials representing counties or cities. The 23 local college boards function more in an advisory capacity to the college president than they would as a board of trustees in another state. From a governance perspective, Virginia's local boards approve establishing and discontinuing academic programs, program advisory committee members, and a small portion of college budgets. Local college board members also serve as ambassadors who advocate for funding with the state legislature, although the chancellor of the VCCS, along with the State Board, is responsible for determining the legislative priorities for every legislative session.

From the Association of Community College Trustees (ACCT):

> In most states, each community college has its own independently operating governing board. In nearly a dozen states, however, a statewide system governs all community and technical colleges. These systems, which are found in 11 states nationwide, offer varying combinations of local and statewide governance, but their leaders say they allow the alignment of statewide priorities and local needs. Most statewide governing bodies are called Boards of Trustees. The titles and number of members of these statewide systems and their leaders indicate their variety.

Based on a 2012 ACCT study:

- 36 states have local governing or advisory boards
- 11 states have state governing boards
- 31 states have boards appointed by the governor
- 14 states have publicly elected boards
- 5 states have a mix of appointed and elected board members
- Virginia has a centralized governance structure, the Virginia Community College System. The VCCS, through its State Board for Community Colleges and Chancellor's Office, hold primary responsibility for the policies, practices, standards, performance, and governance of all 23 Community Colleges. Some of those responsibilities are delegated to or shared with a locally appointed board that acts on behalf of the VCCS through prescribed governance policies. They include approval of curriculum changes,

approval of local budgets, naming of buildings, and others. Ultimately, the responsibility rests with the VCCS through its State Board and chancellor. In Virginia, the local board is a hybrid with little real authority and a role of being advisory instead of governance.

- Pennsylvania has a strong local board governance model. The local board is elected, much like a K–12 school board. It has much more responsibility for local taxes in support of the college and college governance and approving such things as the college budget, hiring of staff, and many other things, since it has neither a chancellor's office nor a state board of authority.

- Rhode Island's eight-member Council on Postsecondary Education has a commissioner who runs the Office of the Postsecondary Commissioner.

- In Washington State, public community and technical colleges have local governing boards. They are co-governed by the nine-member Washington State Board for Community and Technical Colleges (SBCTC), which is headed by an Executive Director.

- The Kentucky Community and Technical College System (KCTCS), which was formed by combining the 14 community colleges of the University of Kentucky and the 15 technical institutes in the Kentucky Workforce Development cabinet, is headed by a system president and governed by a 14-member Board of Regents.

Reference: www.acct.org/article/state-community-college-governance.

Like many other things in life, there can be advantages and disadvantages to being community college president in a statewide community college system. Below are some thoughts from a community college president's perspective about leading a college that is part of a larger system. Also, none of the items discussed below are intended to be criticisms of a large community college system; they are simply dynamics which with the community college president must work regardless of the institution that they lead.

Being college president in a large community college system can bring a sense of greater stability and safety to the president, just as during rough seas riding on an aircraft carrier feels much safer than riding in a speedboat. However, consistent with the metaphor, the aircraft carrier is not as nimble as the speedboat. The carrier takes longer to stop, and if either wants to change direction, the aircraft carrier must make a long sweeping curve while the speedboat can change direction almost on a dime.

The Local Board

Regardless of how the local board is seated, the community college president, faculty, and staff need to recognize the college board's role. Whether an elected or appointed board, the selection is not up to you. That means you may have little influence on the board's makeup, background, tenure, or behavior. Understanding your limits concerning the board's role, responsibilities, and makeup is critical. This is especially true when a misstep can affect revenue contributions from local jurisdictions, alienate local government's leadership, or change the will of the community via the ballot box. Critical missteps can result in reduced financial support or even the removal of the president.

From Dr. Glenn DuBois, Chancellor, Virginia Community College System (VCCS):

> The caring and the feeding of the local board is very important. You don't want to take it for granted. I think that relationship is key. You can have a fabulous relationship with faculty, staff, and students, but if you have a really poor relationship with a board, it's probably terminal.

From James Cuthbertson, Board Member J. Sargeant Reynolds Community College, former State Board Chair, Virginia Community College System (VCCS):

> It is imperative that colleges, universities and college systems populate their governing boards with the most visionary and mission-driven leaders available. Exceptional leaders recognize the value and gifts that others bring to the table; other competent and successful team members do not threaten them. They readily share information and use their influence to advance the careers of their colleagues for the betterment of the organization.
>
> Exceptional leaders are life-long learners and remain accessible and approachable. They are of high moral character and are accountable throughout their board tenure for their actions and decisions. Likewise, they are held to high standards in all their professional endeavors. They are skillful and competent in the art of organizational design and governance.
>
> They have an outward perspective by understanding the role and position they play in the larger cosmos of their discipline, and their stature within the decision-making hierarchy of their respective institutions and higher education systems. By having an outward perspective, exceptional board members are recognizable as visionaries. They acknowledge that the future belongs to

those individuals and organizations that embrace change. Those with vision espouse and chart courses that will move their organization to positions of prominence despite the chaos and risk associated with innovation and departure from the safe status quo. They are the ones who will prevail. Those leaders are the ones who accept the challenges to their organization's safety and continuing success willingly and eagerly. They recognize that the high price of success is often less costly than the price of remaining stagnant in an ever-changing landscape.

So, where does the visionary academic leader go from here? They must acknowledge the changing landscape of higher education and recognize negative forces affecting its success. All of that must be on their institution's docket. The visionary leaders will be academia's change agents. They will challenge conventions and find substantive ways to improve retention and graduation rates, lower student costs, and increase the return on their college's investment.

Visionary board leaders will support the pursuit of innovative and collaborative partnerships with major employers. These opportunities will illuminate new opportunities while they advance mutually shared goals of higher graduation rates and a more skillfully trained workforce. They must get out ahead of the issues. The community colleges that best weather challenging storms are those that anticipate and confront issues early and honestly.

Government Oversight: Federal, State, and Local

Peter Blake, Director State Council of Higher Education for Virginia (SCHEV), offers his insights on government oversight:

A public institution of higher education is part of a larger network of public institutions, and it can be excellent only when it finds its place in that greater framework. All public institutions possess public purposes and contribute to the public good not only by pursuing their own singular goals but also by addressing public needs both individually and collectively. These needs manifest at the state, regional and community levels, often varying greatly across regions and communities. This variation in local needs is reflected in the name "community college."

To be successful in this context, community college presidents and boards must contribute to the development of state goals; communicate the state's goals to the local community; adapt the institution to be a unique contributor to meeting the state's goals; and communicate to the state oversight bodies what the college is doing, what it is observing in its community, and what resources it needs to be even more successful in meeting state's needs.

First, presidents and boards must understand the structure of oversight in the state. Each state oversees public higher education differently, and thus oversees community colleges differently. In seeking to understand this, take a broad view. Beyond the state higher education executive office or offices (SHEEOs), consider the governor and other executive-branch agencies, as well as legislative leadership. These constituencies are not always united in their thinking about the state's needs, goals, priorities and realities, and each body brings different expectations. Effective community college leaders find ways to stitch together the needs of their state "overseers" and demonstrate ways in which their institutions are meeting those overseers' most elemental needs.

Second, presidents and boards must understand their community, the college and the interplay of the two. What are the community's needs, goals, priorities and realities, and how do these factors shape the expectations of community leaders and the general citizenry? What are the community's views on—and formal or informal roles in—postsecondary education and training? Do postsecondary support/access organizations exist in the community, and how successful are they? What are the college's strengths, strategic advantages, limitations, and deficiencies? How do these attributes contribute to the college's reputation, standing and perception at the state level and within the community? What are the college's needs, goals, priorities and realities, and how do these factors contribute to perceptions and expectations?

Once presidents and boards have developed the knowledge above, they will be in a better position to approach the next set of important considerations: their ability and capacity to communicate about and respond to this knowledge.

The more adept presidents and boards are at reaching these understandings, the better positioned and prepared they will be to deploy them to the benefit of the college, the community, and the state. Presidents and boards will have become more skilled advocates both for the college and for the community—while becoming equally strong advocates for the state's needs and goals.

State Influence

Regardless of the governance structure, community colleges are usually dependent on state government and/or local county monies for a significant portion of their revenue outside of tuition. Tuition rates are set and governed at the state or local level. Likewise, in many states, capital projects, construction, land acquisition, and similar functions are managed by the state or local jurisdiction.

The community college board and the president need to understand their role with the state players, including the system office and the system CEO, the Department of Education, the governor, and the legislature. State funding, CEO oversight, curriculum, facilities, service area definition, articulation agreements, and others are the responsibility of the state, or responsibility is shared with the college. Having a clear understanding of your role and its limits is the only way to ensure that everyone is effectively working towards the same goal. In other words, embrace your responsibilities, but be careful not to overstep your authority.

Further thought on the dynamics with vice chancellors and other system office staff from Dr. Monty Sullivan, System President of Louisiana's community and technical colleges:

> There is always going to be tension; I think a healthy tension. When that tension results in what is best for the state as a whole and what is best for localities, you are able to do more for everyone. I spend a lot of time talking with our system office folks about advancing our shared goals and balancing the needs of the states and the localities. In order to succeed in that, there needs to be a high level of trust. That trust really goes both ways; there has to be trust that the system leader is acting in the best interest of the college, and the college leader is acting in the best interest of the system leader, and all parties are acting in the best interests of the students.
>
> I think the final point that I would make is that the relationship between the system leader and the college is critical, and sometimes a hard lesson to learn. One must find a way to be direct without being disrespectful, demeaning, or undermining. That is best accomplished with a long-term relationship that gives you time to get to know each other and recover from inevitable missteps. One of the things I hear back from our system colleges is that they appreciate the fact that they will never have to wonder where they stand with me. That important element allows them to go out into the community and take risks to fulfill their mission. Sometimes they make difficult decisions, but they know that I have their back. The reason they know that is that we have a history of respecting each other and frankly working through difficulties over time.

The Federal Government

Similarly, the federal government plays a significant role in managing the community college via financial aid policies that often affect tuition rates, outcomes and reporting, admission policies for veterans and others, and accreditation. Most of this top-down governance is managed though the U.S. Department of Education. Pell Grants are the most important form of financial aid for community colleges students, helping more than 2.4 million of them access and succeed in higher education each year.

6. Pyramid or Funnel?

The cutting-edge Carl D. Perkins Career and Technical Education Act (CTE) programs are the largest ongoing source of federal institutional support for community colleges. In addition, the Perkins Basic State Grants give postsecondary institutions the flexibility to identify local priorities and fund innovation in occupational education programs. Community colleges use these grants to improve curricula; prepare students for high-skill, in-demand fields by helping them meet challenging academic, vocational, and technical standards; purchase equipment students need to know how to operate in today's jobs; integrate vocational and academic instruction; and foster better links between colleges and the business community.

Internal Constituencies (Shared Governance)

"Shared governance" with internal stakeholders (governance groups)—Faculty Senate, Professional Faculty/Administrative Senate, Classified Council, and Student Senate or Student Council—is typically the mechanism for interaction between college administration and subgroups of employees at the college.

> **The Billboard Says It All: A Faculty Request for Reserved Parking**
>
> It was during my first community college presidency in southern Minnesota that I learned how cold it can actually get during the winter months where there are no mountains, very few hills, and winds that often push south from the even colder neighbor in Canada. Yes, it could be very cold!
>
> One day during a faculty senate meeting the faculty leadership added the topic of "Reserved Parking for Faculty" to our joint agenda. The request included exploring options to have a gated and secure area for faculty parking as close as possible to the entrance of the building. Now just to put things in perspective, it is common in Minnesota for college campuses (as well as commercial buildings) to be connected with enclosed walkways, typically made of glass, so that once a person enters a building they no longer need to walk outside in the cold to get to different parts of the campus. In fact, many parts of downtown Minneapolis, including the Convention Center, are connected with these "skywalks" that enable a person to spend the day getting to and from other buildings without ever having to go outside.

So, what about this faculty request for reserved parking? Although I was new as their college president, during the presidential search process I had emphasized greatly my passion for a culture focused on what was in the students' best interest. I had even gone so far as to publicly express what I often referred to as "our loftiest value statement" being "Is today's decision in the best interest of our students?"

Here is what I did.

At the very next faculty senate meeting I brought the request up again and then asked the question "Faculty, who do you believe are the most important people on campus?" and the faculty shouted out with enthusiasm, "The students!"—the right answer, of course! My response to their request, hoping that they truly believed students were the most important people on campus, was the following:

"If we really believe that our students are the most important people on campus then why don't we have faculty and staff park in the most distant parking lot from the building and place an attractive sign in the lot for everyone to read that would say 'Faculty and staff choose to park in this most distant parking lot because we believe that the students are the most important people on campus!'"

The subject of reserved parking for faculty next to the building entrance was never brought up again....

Unions and Collective Bargaining in Community Colleges

Many colleges employ staff and faculty that are represented by unions or through collective bargaining. This dynamic can affect the relationship between community college presidents, their college boards, and their faculty and staff.

Currently, five, mostly adjacent states—Georgia, North Carolina, South Carolina, Virginia, and Texas—do not allow collective bargaining for teachers. Further, North Carolina, South Carolina, and Virginia have blanket statutes that prohibit collective bargaining for all public-sector employees.

Although one can Google the "advantages and disadvantages of collective bargaining" and easily find lists of pros and cons, it often ultimately boils down to the relationships between "administration" and other employee groups within an institution. These employee groups usually include teaching faculty, classified staff (clerical, maintenance, and grounds workers), and administrative/professional (mid-level managers, librarians, and counselors).

In union environments it would be typical to find a Faculty Union, a Classified Council Union, a Professional/Technical Staff Union, etc. Although the actual names can vary, it would be these formal unions that represent the individuals in each employee group. The union would negotiate a "contract" between the management and the (union) workers that would usually be renewed every four to six years. The "contract" would spell out in detail certain benefits (and their limits) for individual employee groups. In addition, the "contract" usually defines a process that would be followed whenever there is a significant disagreement between workers and administration. In other words, the "contract" would define the workers' rights as employees.

It is also worth pointing out that there can be significant differences in the cultures of different union relationships. The extreme example would be that of "traditional" labor collective bargaining versus "interest-based" collective bargaining. The traditional bargaining culture is one, now considered old fashioned, that is often polarized with "management" against "labor" and in which both sides bring in their "want lists" and negotiate back and forth until they can reach a compromise. The more modern, interest-based bargaining approach is more collaborative. It often requires the management and labor work together (sometimes for a year or more before actual negotiations begin), get to know each other, build relationships and trust, and communicate interests of workers and administrators so they can do their best to identify "win-win" opportunities in the negotiation process.

Although there are exceptions to the rule, most college presidents and their boards will find that the pathway to success is often similar for union and non-union colleges because the fundamental principles of effective leadership enable success. Fairness, collaboration, and transparency, with frequent and honest communication, make for successful relationships.

Litigation and the Perception of a State with Deep Pockets

Every business can find itself threatened from time-to-time with a lawsuit from someone who thinks he/she deserves restitution for something. In a large statewide community college system, it is often the state

Attorney General's Office that provides lawyers to work on behalf of the system and individual colleges when litigation becomes necessary. Some people who want to abuse the state system for personal gain perceive the state as having "deep pockets," and for whatever reason if things cannot be worked out over an issue, a lawsuit ensues. We mention this here because state attorneys will often settle before a suit goes to trial, with the logic that it would cost the state much more in time and money if it were to pursue the trial than to settle out of court.

This can be very frustrating for the college president as it puts their college in the position of having to pay possibly tens of thousands of dollars to someone who, for all realistic purposes, is gaming the system. That being said, it is part of life!

System Office Staff Understanding the Cadence of Life on a Community College Campus

Most staff who work out of a statewide system office are centralized in a location with similar colleagues. Although most system office staff have experience working on a community college campus, some do not. Statewide system offices are bureaucratic operations that differ greatly from the operations and cadence of a community college campus.

It is certainly a great advantage if staff who work at a system office are familiar enough with life on the actual campus that they consider the impact that their work can have on the campus faculty, staff, and students. For example, the most stressful time for teaching faculty and students is near the end of the semester and it would be very appreciated if system office staff did not create new and/or additional work during those few weeks.

A sound practice for chancellors and presidents of statewide systems is to require all system office staff spend a few days a year on a community college campus in some capacity that helps college faculty and staff get to know them (and vice versa). They will also see firsthand the dynamics of what happens on a campus, so they can better relate to the impact of any actions they might make.

The Frustration of Unfunded Mandates

Whether an unfunded mandate comes from the governor's office or the community college system office, it is usually burdensome for the college president and their staff, especially if the college leadership has not been part of the dialogue and development from concept to implementation.

Typically, governors want to create and establish their own legacy. So, it's not unusual for an incoming governor to be disinclined to continue funding or expanding the initiative of the previous governor. As the result, a common and challenging scenario is for the state (through the governor's office) to develop a new program, direct a college to implement the program, and provide funding for just two to three years. Later, they leave the community college in the position of stopping the program or finding other resources on its own to keep it going. One can image that over a period of years the costs of such programs continue to compound on each other, and they can deplete monies from other areas of need of the college.

This dynamic can also play out in statewide community college systems. System office staff diligently secure grants, take an indirect cost fee off the top, assign the project to one or more of the colleges, and then let the college staff add to their plates the additional workload for the new, exciting program. And then ... once the source of funding ends, the college will need to find a way to continue the program through its own budget.

Audits and Compliance ... "Tone at the Top"

Whit Madère
Former Director of Internal Audit,
Virginia Community College System

Perhaps the most important thing for any leader to know about internal auditors is that they are conditioned to look for the "tone at the top" of any organization. The principles of effective internal control begin with the control environment, and that environment begins with leadership that demonstrates a commitment to integrity and ethical values.

Audit and Compliance are two different and distinct roles in any organization, but they are often mistaken for the same thing. We think of our managers and management controls as the first line of defense for making sure all employees do the right things in a culture of compliance. The compliance officer or team is the second line of defense, along with the financial controller, security, risk management team and others. They are charged with monitoring activities and controls to reasonably ensure that the company is complying with all applicable laws, rules and regulations, as well as internal codes of conduct, policies, and procedures. The internal audit function evaluates the internal control environment throughout the organization to ensure adequacy of controls as well as organizational efficiency and effectiveness. Internal audit is the third line of defense, and it performs audits of compliance, finance, security and other all other functions. In this chapter, we will not focus on organizational structure at your college; rather, the discussion will center on attitudes toward these oversight functions as well as the president's relationship with your lead auditor or compliance officer.

Unfortunately, for some organizations the thought of being visited by an auditor evokes some painful memories from past audits. When working with internal auditors, the relationship does not need to be a contentious or unpleasant one. The key word that many people forget about internal auditors is that first word, *internal*, which serves as a reminder us that your internal auditor is a part of *your* team.

Core Values in the Relationship

To be clear, auditors must be independent and objective. They are sometimes tasked with delivering bad news, but that can actually help lead to a stronger and healthier organization. To that end, it is important to build a relationship with your auditor that is founded on core values of sincerity, integrity, and courage. Of those three values, sincerity might be the one that is most often overlooked, but it might be the most important in the auditor's relationship with leaders.

Sincerity is about genuineness, freedom from hypocrisy or ulterior motives. It is more about our *intentions* than about what we actually say or do. In other words, it is the "why" behind our actions. A sincere relationship between leader and auditor is paramount to establishing a strong relationship. The auditor may have to deliver bad news, but it should never be to get the president or others in trouble; it should be to help the organization to improve—in all sincerity. The leader, likewise, should be willing to ask for guidance or opinions from the auditor, and should sincerely want to hear even the hardest answers that might be given.

While sincerity is essential to the leader-auditor relationship, it is nothing without integrity. Integrity connotes more than just honesty, but honesty is most important. Integrity also means an adherence to strong moral or ethical principles, and between the leader and auditor, every conversation should be honest and complete, withholding none of the significant facts.

Sometimes it takes courage to deliver and to ask for the hard facts. At times there may be consequences for the auditor, the leader, or the organization, but both the leader and the auditor need to have to courage to face those consequences for the good of the organization. Just as with your doctor or lawyer, you should always expect honesty from your auditor, no matter how unpleasant the news might be.

Mustard—It's About Sincerity

Once, as an adjunct faculty member teaching and auditing class in the evenings, I was running a little late commuting from my job to the college. There was little time to stop to eat, so I pulled into a fast-food restaurant and got a hamburger to eat while I was driving. When I got to the college, I rushed into the classroom and began the class without a minute to spare.

After an hour and fifteen minutes of lecturing, we took the regularly scheduled break, and I went to the restroom, looked in the mirror, and saw that I had mustard on my chin. I wondered why none of the 24 students in the class had bothered to say anything to me about it. I asked them, and for the next hour and fifteen minutes of that class period, we talked about the responsibilities of the auditor and the need to be willing to share bad news.

When I asked the class who had noticed the mustard on my chin, all of their hands went up. Then I asked them why no one had bothered to mention it. One student remarked, "we didn't want to embarrass you in front of the whole class." That answer did not satisfy me, as the embarrassment was still there when I looked in the mirror. I don't think it was really about saving *me* the embarrassment, as everyone *except me* knew about the mustard. I think the real answer is that no one in the class wanted to call attention to himself or herself by being the one to point out the problem that was obvious to everyone.

How often do leaders sit in front of their leadership teams with a new challenge or a new idea ... and mustard on their chins? Sometimes, even if everyone in the room can see something, and they have reason to believe that everyone else sees the same thing, they hold back for fear of embarrassing or challenging the leader, or drawing attention to themselves as "the one who spoke out."

Now I wondered how much I could trust any of the students in my class to tell me the hard truth. When the college leader discovers later that there was mustard that everyone else could see, but no one spoke up, that leader might wonder how much he or she can trust the rest of the leadership team.

I imagine that if the classroom I walked into had been full of seventh graders instead of college students, there might have been snickering and pointing. Someone might have pointed out the mustard specifically to embarrass me and make fun of me. That would be a lack of *sincerity*, even though it showed honesty and courage. On the other hand, if I am about to walk out of my house to go to work, my wife would point out the mustard—not to get a laugh, but because she genuinely cares to keep me from being embarrassed later.

Auditors need all three values—sincerity, integrity and courage—to effectively serve the college and its president. Similarly, the president should demonstrate all three of those values in their relationship with the auditor. When you, as the leader, are getting ready to walk out on stage or in front of the cameras, you should get checked out by the makeup artist first. Make it a point to have your auditor take one last look to see whether there is mustard on your chin.

About Fences—Control Boundaries

At an elementary school, a playground adjacent to the school had a tall chain link fence around it, and at recess time the students were allowed to play anywhere in the enclosed area, including right up against the fence. Due to some road and sidewalk construction the fence had to be temporarily taken down. Rather than keeping the children inside for recess, the teachers were instructed to just keep a close eye on them so that they did not stray too far away from the building. What they found was that all of the children seemed to huddle very close to the building during recess, because they did not know exactly how far they were allowed to go.

The fence is an internal control. It sets a boundary, but it can make people feel safe if they stay within that boundary. Employees

6. Pyramid or Funnel?

need boundaries, too. By erecting the fences and making them visible, employees will have a better understanding of how far they can go in any direction. Consider whether your organization has "invisible" fences like the type used to keep pets in a certain area. The pets don't feel the unpleasant effect of the fence's shock or warning sound until they have gone too far.

Some critics of invisible fences say that they are only about 70 percent effective and can make dogs more reactive and aggressive.

That is not what you want for your employees, so work with your internal auditor to make sure everyone can *see* the fences. Talk about them openly and regularly. Make sure your employees and auditors know how to respond when someone kicks a ball over the fence, then use it as an opportunity to talk about what direction the kickers should be facing when playing kickball in the future. When it makes sense, explore whether the fenced in area can be or should be expanded or contracted. Most importantly, create an environment that embraces the controls rather than instilling fear of them. Your employees, like the students at the school, will play right up to the fence without fear of going a little too far and getting shocked.

Shoulder Pads and Helmets: Protecting Your Team So They Can Play Faster

Football players in the United States did not start wearing the protective equipment we see today until after decades of injuries. In fact, while some players wore optional leather skullcaps in the early 1900s, plastic helmets were not made mandatory until around 1939. Leather shoulder pads did not evolve into the hard, plastic pads we see today until the 1960s. Some players objected to the mandatory use of protective equipment, fearing they would be encumbered, their movements restricted, and the game slowed down. If fact, the game has sped up because players have more confidence that the equipment will protect them.

As pointed out earlier in this chapter, part of the president's role is to create a culture of safety. Working without following internal controls is like taking the field without your shoulder pads. The rules, controls, and auditors are not there to slow you down; rather, they are there to help you speed up. The leader-auditor relationship is important to protect students and employees, not just physically, but in other ways as well. Think of the college president as the coach and the auditor as the equipment manager. The auditor can inspect the equipment to make sure it is sound but cannot make the players wear it. The coach calls the plays and sends in the players... but insists that they will not play without their shoulder pads and helmets.

Perspectives on Longhorn Cows

Growing up in Texas, everyone understands that there is a rivalry between the Texas Longhorns and the Texas A&M Aggies. The Longhorn mascot is a full-sized longhorn cow, and such longhorns can be seen in fields and ranchlands all across Texas. I remember driving home and seeing a longhorn grazing in the field, so I pulled over to take a picture. There was a burnt orange (the school color) sunset behind the animal, and it looked up and turned its head toward me. The massive horns paralleled the horizon, and I thought to myself, "What a majestic creature. How could anyone *not* be a Longhorn fan?"

I still have a picture like the one I took in the field hanging in my office. Whenever I look at it, I am reminded that there might just as easily have been an Aggie in that field, working and feeding the cow. The Aggie would have seen the cow from the other side, and the burnt orange light would have shown on the backside of the cow with its tail chasing away flies. The Aggie might have remarked "This is a smelly and ugly creature. How could anyone be a Longhorn fan?"

The truth is that both perspectives are 100 percent accurate, but neither of them is 100 percent complete. As a leader, you will want to understand the whole animal, and not just the part that looks good, or the part that looks bad and smells. The role of the auditor is not to paint a two-dimensional picture of the cow; rather, it is to produce a life-sized replica of the whole animal, so that the leader can walk around it, climb over it, or crawl under it—to see it as it really is.

As a college president, you can show your willingness to embrace the whole cow by being willing to walk out in the field with your auditor. Sometimes, it is messy, and you might get your feet dirty, but others on your team will notice your commitment and they will be willing to follow your example. When your employees vehemently argue that they have a different view of the cow, acknowledge the value of their perspectives, but encourage them to recognize that others have valid perspectives too.

6. Pyramid or Funnel?

Conclusion

This topic began with the "tone at the top," and that phrase encompasses two important elements. One is the "top." Your employees and team see *you* as the top at your college. The other element is "tone," and it is important to point out that *silence is not a tone*. Don't take the mistaken position that if no one ever hears about internal audit or compliance, then everything must be working well. Instead, make compliance and controls a normal part of the conversation and culture of your organization.

As the president, be willing to bring those with the most opposite or competing views into the same room at the same time. The greater the disparity of perspectives, the greater the potential value of the outcome. When you have the whole team together, including your audit and compliance professionals, be brave enough to acknowledge the mustard on others' chins, and empower them to acknowledge yours. Talk about your fences, and make sure everyone can see them and knows what to do if the ball flies over a fence. Encourage your people to use the controls to help them play faster and harder, but always wearing the proper gear or armed with the processes and controls that are designed to let them play fearlessly. Finally, keep looking for those around you that have a different perspective of the cow—and keep the cycle going.

Your audit and compliance professionals can be among your greatest assets, so never hesitate to include them in the most important conversations amongst your advisors and the most important decisions that you make. Be sincere, honest, and courageous with them, and ask that be sincere, honest, and courageous with you.

Key Chapter Takeaways

- Remember the Serenity Prayer; it will afford much comfort.
- Honest and fair communications are critical to all relationships.
- Win-win results foster sustainable partnerships.
- Know who your bosses are.
- If part of a state-wide community college system, accept the relationship with open eyes and an understanding of the positive and negatives of being part of a large system.
- Audits can be very helpful to an institution and the potential for win-wins is significantly influenced by the tone at the top.

Chapter 7

Why Didn't You Read the Instructions?

The Need for a Complete College Board Policy Manual

Need for a Board Manual

We've all done it. We've unpacked the pieces of the exercise machine; we look at the picture on the box and we start assembling.

Sometimes it works out. Sometimes it doesn't. You might end up with some "extra" parts. You might not have properly assembled the safety features. After a mishap, reluctantly you pick up the instructions. In big letters on the first page you see "READ THE INSTRUCTIONS FIRST!"

Now you tell me.

College board members should not jump in without preparation. The job is too important. The lack of preparation and inevitable mistakes may have implications with long or permanent impacts. New college board member preparation requires proper orientation anchored by a comprehensive College Board Manual. In addition, the College Board Manual is essential for proper execution of board member duties throughout their tenure.

A typical board manual contains:

- A letter of introduction to the board members from the chair and the college president
- Board bylaws
- Expectations of a board member
- Board policies
- New board member orientation
- Board events
- Board manual revision log

7. Why Didn't You Read the Instructions?

What follows is a detail of the key components of a complete College Board Manual.

Sample Letter of Introduction

Dear College Board,

We wish to welcome you to the _____ Community College Board and provide you with this <u>College Board Manual</u> that will serve as a tool to make your experience as a Board member more successful.

The _____ College Board plays an important governance and advisory role for _____ Community College and board members serve as the eyes and ears of the jurisdictions they represent in assisting the college president in leading the college. Our shared goal is to serve our communities by preparing its citizens for life and for careers through college programs and services.

This manual has been created to provide you with information related to the role of _____ Community College in our community and policies that clarify how the College Board functions in its efforts to support the college.

As you execute your Board duties, we hope that you will reflect upon the charge that each of the _____ Community College faculty and staff uses to help guide them through their duties:

Is today's decision in the best interest of our students?

Thank you for serving the _____ Community College Board, our college, our community, and our students.

[College Board Chair]   *[College President]*

Board Bylaws

Board bylaws describe the board and cover how the board operates. The bylaws should:

Define the board and its authority

"The State Board shall establish policies providing for the creation of a local community college board for each institution established under this chapter and the procedures and regulations under which such local boards shall operate. A local community college board as defined in § 23-214 shall be established for each college. These boards shall assist in ascertaining educational needs, enlisting community involvement and support, and shall perform such other duties as may be prescribed by the State Board" (1966, c. 679).

Define the board's purpose

- The college board is committed to and supports the college's vision, mission, and values.
- The college board members will be good stewards of resources and make effective and efficient use of them, thereby ensuring accountability to the Commonwealth and to the communities it serves.
- The board members will maintain the confidentiality and security of information entrusted to it and share information only when authorized or required by law to do so.
- The board members will not accept any gift, favor, loan, service, business or professional opportunity from anyone knowing (or in a position indicating they should know) that it is offered in order to improperly influence the performance of its public duties.
- The board members will avoid even the appearance of a conflict of interest, and will offer good faith and fair dealings to all those it serves and with each other.

Define the board's makeup

The State Board for Community Colleges hereby established the following service region for J. Sargeant Reynolds Community College: the City of Richmond, and the Counties of Goochland, Hanover, Henrico, Louisa (shared with Piedmont Virginia Community College), and Powhatan. The board shall consist of fifteen (15) members. The City of Richmond and the County of Henrico shall have five (5) representatives each, while the County of Hanover shall have two (2) representatives,

7. Why Didn't You Read the Instructions?

and the Counties of Goochland, Louisa, and Powhatan shall have one (1) representative each.

Describe how board members are selected, appointed, removed, and/or replaced

The members of the college board shall be residents of the region to be served by the community college and shall include persons from various businesses, industries, and professions in the region being served by the community college. No elected members of either the General Assembly or of a local governing body shall be eligible to serve on the college board; however, elected town officials shall not be prohibited from serving on a college board so long as such town is not a participating political subdivision sponsoring the college. All members of the college board shall be deemed members at large charged with the responsibility of serving the best interests of the whole region being served by the community college.

Members shall be appointed for a term of four (4) years. In accordance with policy of the State Board for Community Colleges, the anniversary date of members of the board is July 1. No person having served on the college board for two (2) successive four-year terms shall be eligible for reappointment to the college board for two (2) years. However, a person appointed to fill an unexpired term may serve two (2) additional successive terms.

Describe how matters before the board are decided

A quorum of members is defined as a majority of sitting board members. A quorum is required to hold a meeting and approve any board actions. Board actions will be managed by the board chair in accordance with Roberts Rules of Order.

Cover procedures for board meeting public access, closed sessions, publication of minutes, and other public facing issues

The college board will meet at least six (6) times per year (July through June) on the first Thursday of the month at a time designated by the chair. An approved schedule of board meeting dates for the year will be provided. Public notice of all meetings must occur two weeks prior.

All meetings shall have approved minutes approved and available for public review.

Define the board's organization

The officers of the college board shall be a chair and vice chair/chair-elect. The president of the college serves as secretary to the board.

The officers of the board shall be elected every year at the regular meeting of the college board in June or as needed to fill a vacancy. The term of office shall be for one (1) year. The chair and vice chair/chair-elect are eligible to serve two (2) consecutive terms.

The chair shall:

- plan and chair meetings;
- ensure that actions by the board are implemented as needed;
- sign approved documents on behalf of the board;
- perform other duties as needed to ensure the college board is running effectively and in accordance with its duties and responsibilities as prescribed by the VCCS.

The vice-chair/chair-elect shall:

- assist the chair in ensuring that the agreed tasks and functions of the board are carried out;
- perform chair duties as needed.

Officers of the college board may be removed from office by a vote of the majority of the total membership of the college board.

Define the board committees

EXECUTIVE COMMITTEE

The executive committee has the authority to act on matters requiring action before the next regularly scheduled college board meeting. The board chair will chair the committee and may call the committee to convene as actions demand. The chair, vice chair/chair-elect, immediate past board chair, and chairs of the standing committees are members; the college president will provide staff support.

PRESIDENT'S EVALUATION COMMITTEE

The president's evaluation committee will be responsible for the

7. Why Didn't You Read the Instructions?

president's annual evaluation that will be submitted to the college board for approval at the April board meeting.

College Board Nominating Committee

The college board nominating committee's purpose is to provide recommendations for board officers to the college board for consideration to fill positions as needed.

Finance and Facilities Committee

The finance and facilities committee will review the college's state budget and all local funds and audits. Results of these reviews will be briefed to the college board with appropriate recommendations. The committee will also review all capital outlay projects, regardless of funding sources, and make appropriate recommendations to the college board. The committee will also track the progress of strategic goals for the comprehensive strategic plan and report its findings to the college board. The board chair may assign other planning items. The vice president of finance and administration will provide staff support.

Academic, Student Affairs, and Workforce Development Committee

The academic, student affairs, and workforce development committee will review, when required, all instructional offerings (both credit and non-credit) and make appropriate recommendations to the college board. The chair of the college's curriculum committee will serve as an ex-officio member of the committee. Both the vice president of academic affairs and the vice president of student affairs will provide staff support.

Board Operations and Planning Committee

The board operations and planning committee will plan and support board activities and develop the next generation of board leadership. To accomplish this the committee will:
- review and revise the board manual, as needed;
- review and improve the board orientation, development plan, and other board member activities, including planning and implementing the annual college board retreat:
- develop advocacy and partnerships;
- support and contribute to the college's planning and institutional effectiveness.

Describe the process for amending the bylaws

These bylaws may be amended, enlarged, or repealed at any meeting of the board, provided at least ten (10) days prior to such meeting, the secretary of the board, or the secretary's designee deliver electronically to each member of the board at the address reflected in the books of the secretary, a copy of the proposed amendment, enlargement, or repeal. Said copy shall also state the reasons justifying the proposal, and the date and place for its consideration. At the meeting wherein the proposal is considered by the board, the board shall have the authority and power to adopt the proposal in any form it shall then see fit, provided a quorum is present. Any member of the board may waive the right to the notice herein provided at any time and under such conditions as the member shall see fit. The provisions of these bylaws shall go into effect upon adoption. As of their effective dates, these provisions shall supersede all prior actions of the board which are inconsistent with them.

Expectations of a Board Member

When you are considering becoming a college board member, it is helpful to know in advance what you are getting into. Furthermore, if the position is appointed, a list of responsibilities can be helpful to those who are considering candidates.

What follows is an example of board member expectations to consider.

Support the community college mission and principles

College board members must understand and accept that their primary purpose of serving on the board is to support the mission of the community college, the values of the college, and support the president at the board level.

Attend the new board member orientation

New board members will be invited to attend a new board orientation, which is an informative session designed to assist in developing insight and understanding essential to performance as a member of the college board.

Strive for exemplary attendance to board meetings

Six board meetings are held between September and June each year. In addition, a joint meeting of the college and foundation boards is held once a year.

Serve on at least one standing committee

Each board member is expected to serve on at least one standing committee. Preferences will be taken into consideration. These committees will meet as scheduled, usually three to six times a year. The dates and times are scheduled as agreed upon by committee members.

Attend key events

Throughout the year, a number of events occur that board members should make every effort to attend. They include, but are not limited to, graduation, convocation, the annual scholarship luncheon, and the board retreat.

Help in "friend-raising"

- Board members are asked to make presentations and personal calls to tell the college's story.
- Board members are asked to make contacts with local and state officials, as well as business and community leaders, to advance the goals of the college.
- College board members are expected to serve as their county or city representative to the college by serving as a conduit for communication between their locality and the college.

Support the community college educational foundation efforts

Board members are encouraged to consider donating to the college's Annual Fund, which supports projects of the highest priority for the college when state funding is insufficient. We realize that some of board members may be in a position to give more, and others cannot do as much, but what is most important is that board members include the college in their philanthropic giving. In addition, members should be encouraged to give consideration to supporting future capital and endowment initiatives, which help to advance the work of the college in the community. Giving can suit every budget, and, properly planned, can help the donor as well as the college.

Assist in ensuring a smooth transition at the conclusion of your term

Board members can assist the college board in a smooth transition at the conclusion of their terms by working with the government body that appointed them several months prior to leaving the board. Although the actual decision resides with the governing body, the governing bodies frequently welcome suggestions from retiring board members who are more familiar with the expectations of the position. A board member can suggest individuals to the governing body that would effectively serve the college as board members.

Board Policies

Board policies describe rules under which the college must operate. Specifically, they describe a behavior with its rationale, limits, and procedures. What follows is a sample board policy to help illustrate its construction.

Statement of purpose policy

Effective	Last Revision	Next Review
Jan 1, 2015	July 1, 2018	June 30, 2020

Purpose

To describe the purpose and process for reviewing and approving the "statement of purpose" of the college.

Policy

The college board's review and approval of the college's statement of purpose (aka mission) is to ensure it is compatible with the state system and local college missions and for subsequent adoption by the state system as described in the State Policy Manual:

7. Why Didn't You Read the Instructions?

The College Board shall participate, with the college president, the Chancellor and the State Board, in the development and evaluation of a program of community college education of high quality in accordance with procedures adopted by the State Board. In that context, a college statement of purpose shall be developed by the college community. It shall be approved by the College Board and reviewed and approved by the Chancellor on behalf of the State Board.

Policy Limits

The college board will evaluate and approve any changes to the college's statement of purpose (mission).

Procedures

The president will periodically review and revise as needed the college's statement of purpose (mission). The president will present the revised statement for review, advisement, and approval by motion of the college board before presenting it to the state board for final review.

New Board Member Orientation

It is not fair to a new college board member to be thrown into the first board meeting without some orientation. Instead, develop a new board member orientation process to help give the new board member a good start. Community colleges are complex organizations with many moving parts. A little work upfront can help diminish the learning curve and assist the new board member in contributing from day one. What follows is an outline of a typical new board member orientation.

New board members are encouraged to participate in the college board member orientation process designed to:

- Welcome them to the board
- Familiarize them with college campuses
- Familiarize them with the College organization, mission, vision, values, and strategic plan
- Help them prepare for their new roles and responsibilities

The orientation process will be the responsibility of the college board chair, who may seek assistance where needed. The process would ideally occur before the new member's first board meeting.

The secretary of the college board will distribute the following information (in hard or electronic copy as applicable) to the new board member:

- The College Board Manual
- College board events calendar
- List of college board members with contact information
- College mission, vision, values, and strategic plan
- College faculty and staff organizational chart
- Directory of president's executive cabinet
- Jurisdiction speaking points and fact sheets
- College course catalog
- Other relevant materials as needed

The chair of the college board will coordinate the following orientation activities:

- Introductory lunch with the chair and president
- Review of the documents provided
- Introduction and training in the use of board member technology aids
- Campus tours with the president

Board Events

In addition to formal board activities, like board meetings, colleges have many different types of events. Having good representation from the college board at many of these events shows support for the college to the community, the faculty and staff, the students, and the president. Providing an outline of these activities gives the board members a sense of the critical events in which they should strive to participate (see illustration next page).

Board Manual Revisions and Review

Annually, in June (for a July fiscal start), the College Board Manual should have been reviewed and revised as needed.

7. Why Didn't You Read the Instructions?

Event	Purpose	When	Attendance Need
Board Meetings	• Take action on board responsibilities • Get updates on college from staff & faculty • Get committee report updates	6 times a year, Sep to Jun	High
Board Retreat	• Learn board roles and responsibilities • Get to know board members • Update annual goals	Early Aug	High
Graduation	Represent College Board	May	High
Convocation	• Update on state of the college • Meet faculty and staff	Oct	High
Local Officials Dinner	• Meet/thank local officials & school superintendents • Spouses/Guest of board member is welcome	Nov	High
Foundation Scholarship Luncheon	Acknowledge scholarship recipients and benefactors	Oct	Med
VCCS Legislative Reception	Represent college with VCCS and state legislators	Jan	Med
Committee Meetings	Work on committee responsibilities	3/6 times year	Med
State Board Annual Meeting	• Represent college with VCCS • Attend board development educational sessions	Nov	Low
College Recognition & Awards Event	Celebrate staff and faculty accomplishments	Apr	Low
Scholarship Bowl	Support classified council scholarship fundraising	Feb	Low

The College Board Manual should include a detail of revisions and modifications to help track its changes over time.

Date	Purpose
March 1, 2018	Amended Presidential Evaluation policy
Nov 10, 2016	New Board Member Orientation process
Feb 6, 2016	Policy updates
July 1, 2015	Amended bylaws; added ten new policies; revised board goals
Sep 8, 2014	Added local visits to Board Events Calendar

Key Chapter Takeaways

- It is important to properly equip board members to exercise their duties. A board manual is the important first step.
- Another critical step is to institute a formal new board member orientation.

Community College Leadership

- Board manuals should be reviewed with new board members as part of their orientation.
- Board manuals should be living documents. A process to regularly review and revise it annually is a part of the board responsibilities.

CHAPTER 8

Relationships, Relationships, Relationships

*Community Engagement
and Leveraging Partnerships*

The Significance of the Word "Community" in Community College

The word "community" in the name of any community college (whether the college is named after a place, a person, or something else) emphasizes the primary purpose of the college: to serve the local community. Each community college has a different character reflective of the community in the immediate college service area. Within a multi-campus college, each campus will likely have slightly different cultural traits—just as three children in the same family will have different personalities—and the campus personality will reflect the neighborhoods surrounding the campus.

Leveraging Community Engagement and the College President

A major role of the community college president is to be the primary "leader of leveraging" of winning relationships. The president is the face of the college for the public and the local community. The president serves as the bridge to relationships and partnerships with community thought leaders, business leaders/employers, community civic groups, the faith-based community, non-profit organizations, K–12 leaders, university partners, and all others that together make up a community.

Why is leveraging relationships with other organizations and community leaders so very important? Simply stated, the importance relates to college mission and economics. Since community colleges generally do not receive the higher level of funding that four-year colleges and universities do, and typically don't have large endowments nor profitable athletics like some universities, the community college president must embrace partnerships throughout its local community and create relationships that result in leveraging resources and joint success.

To be more precise, it is important that the community college president not only engage the thought leaders of the community, but also evolve as quickly as possible into *being* one of the key thought leaders. An indication of this evolution is when the college president begins to be invited to serve on prominent boards or committees or join community groups that drive the success of a community.

One caution, however, is that the timing of this can be very important and challenging.

With a new college president who is from outside of the community, there initially may be numerous invitations for engagement by outside groups. It is wise for the president to be cautious about raising his/her hand to volunteer to join a board or group until enough time has passed for the president to assess the reputation of the organization and explore what the potential and opportunities might be. This can be tricky since new presidents want to create that positive first impression and are also enthusiastic about engaging with other community leaders. Be guided by the following key principle: "It is better to do a few things well than many things poorly!"

Who's Who? Identifying Key Community Stakeholders

Depending on whether the college is located in a small rural town, a mid-size city, or a large urban metropolitan area, the nature of the community college's engagement with thought leaders can be very different. In almost every instance, however, the new president will be able to build upon relationships already developed by the previous president.

The "spheres of influence" in the community can be easily identified by major community projects of recent past, current initiatives (underway or planned), and public communications about the future of the community. The community college president should study the

8. Relationships, Relationships, Relationships

community's priorities to determine which priorities might offer opportunities for the college to engage and become a meaningful partner. After all, it is important that college resources be invested in those initiatives with the greatest possible impact on the lives of students, on their families, and on the community as a whole.

 It is important to build relationships when you do not need anything from people.

If the only time others in the community see you is when you have your hand out, they will quickly learn to run the other way when they see you coming.

If your attitude is more of open arms, willingness to help, potential partners/donors will more likely greet you with open arms when they see you coming!

Provided below are the perspectives of business stakeholders, K–12 education leaders, and the faith community regarding potential for creating partnerships with a local community college.

Business Community Involvement

THEODORE RASPILLER
President, Brightpoint Community College

- **Provide the prepared workforce**—Businesses look to community colleges to provide a skilled workforce that meets the employment needs in the region.
- **Upgrade current employee skills**—Community colleges can partner with the HR/Training Department of local employers to upgrade current employees' knowledge and skills.
- **Co-sponsor education & training**—Businesses can benefit by co-sponsoring employee training with the community college, as employees would see this as an investment in their future by their company as well.
- **Presidential business community leadership**—The college president would benefit the college by serving in a leadership role such as in the local Chamber of Commerce, preferably being on

the Executive Committee of the chamber and even chairing the chamber board of directors.

Perspective of a Hospital CEO

Patrick Farrell
Past President, Henrico Doctors' Hospital, Richmond, Virginia

Community colleges and healthcare organizations would seem to fit together naturally. Hospitals and health systems need qualified staff, which community colleges can help train, and the community colleges need resources, educators, and clinical sites in which to train their students.

However, even though it would seem like a natural fit, partnerships between community colleges and their local healthcare providers may not develop organically. Often, there needs to be a catalyst. It may be a nursing shortage that prompts the local hospital to approach the community college. It may be the community college's acute need for a clinical site to accommodate its students. In the absence of such a catalyst, how should community colleges forge these relationships?

Be the catalyst. The most effective approach is to develop relationships before an acute need arises. Community college leadership must proactively seek out their counterparts in the local healthcare community to identify needs and to articulate the benefits of a close working relationship/partnership.

Approaching a large healthcare organization can be a challenge; these organizations are complex and often bureaucratic. Who should you work with, and at what level in the organization should you initiate contact? As a rule, initiate contact as high in the organizational hierarchy possible. If you are working with a national organization, try to determine the most influential executives who live and work in your community; they can be advocates for you within their organization.

If you do not have a relationship with any executive-level managers (the C-suite), focus on HR or Nursing Administration. Do not be shy about using your network, such as board members, donors, graduates, and community leaders to make introductions. You would be surprised at how many people are willing to help if you just ask.

On the community college side, many individuals beyond the college president may be involved in establishing and maintaining relationships. The dean of the nursing program, VP of development, and faculty working with a clinical facility are all potential contact points, but the role of the president is vital.

Many community college/hospital relationships begin with the establishment of clinical training sites. The hospital provides the students with clinical rotations in their facilities and typically provides adjunct faculty and preceptors for the students. These clinical rotations allow students to gain required clinical experience, and they give the hospital a chance to meet and get to know potential future employees. It easily develops into a win-win.

Establishing a clinical rotation site is a great opportunity to develop a close relationship with the hospital. It is critical, however, that the community college be sensitive to the needs of the hospital and is responsive to feedback. The college leadership must develop a solid understanding of what it takes for a new hire to be successful and incorporate those skills into the curriculum. Responsiveness on the part of the community college can cement the relationship; likewise, if the community college is seen as dismissive, the relationship can quickly sour. Once again, the key is open communication.

Perspective of a Chamber of Commerce CEO

Kim Scheeler

Past President, Chamber RVA

As we look to the future and the role that the community college plays in the preparation of our workforce, engagement with the business community becomes increasingly important. The workforce needs of businesses are evolving at an ever-increasing pace and skill-specific education is becoming a much greater factor in the most desired applicants.

One of the benefits of a community college system is that it typically can be more nimble than a four-year degree program at the universities. One thing we consistently hear from business leaders is that the workforce of the future is going to focus more on specific talents and certifications, and less on general four-year degrees.

While most presidents will have a college board and a foundation board which will include business leaders among their ranks, over time those participants become accustomed to the traditional offerings and practices of a community college. By engaging with the more general business community on a regular basis, the president has the opportunity to hear about frustrations and needs that might not be brought to the table by their most trusted advisors. It is a sort of stealth market research that can be very helpful to the creative president. By understanding trends in workforce needs of the businesses, the visionary president can build non-traditional programs to meet those needs.

In addition to the Chamber of Commerce, there are many opportunities for someone to build relationships in the business community. If your community has an organization of key business leaders, that is a table to join. In addition, downtown partnership organizations can be beneficial. The key is to identify where the business leaders gather, and then get involved in those organizations. Building relationships is the basis for long-term success in any community.

It is important in the engagement in those organizations to learn and contribute. By contribute, I mean to participate in meaningful strategic conversations that will benefit the organization, not just the community college. Everyone recognizes the person at the table whose only concern is his/her own (or the organization's) self-interest. Over time, those players are tuned out and discounted by the rest of the group. The relationship building value comes in when you willingly help the organization in which you are volunteering and others see that benefit accrue to that organization. When you become a valued partner at the table of multiple community organizations, others tend to want to know more about your organization, and the willingness to help you tends to grow.

One other activity that can build a strong network of supporters is that of reaching out to new leaders in your community and inviting them to a lunch, simply to welcome them to the area or welcome them to a new position. Most people greatly appreciate someone reaching out to them and helping them learn a little about the lay of the land when they are new to a community. Those early relationships tend to endure as individuals grow in their positions.

This gives the president and the board the ability to reach out to the business community and gather input as they strive to remain relevant in the world of changing workforce needs. If you ask the business leaders for their input and then use their advice to craft programs that meet their needs, you will eventually build a relationship in which the business leaders turn to the community college when they have needs that they don't know how to address.

Businesses have several challenges in front of them. Workforce shortages will be ramping up at an accelerating pace in the near future (barring an economic downturn) so speed to market of potential employees becomes critical. And, in the high growth areas like technology, there is more interest in job-specific skill training (certification) than someone achieving a bachelor's degree in general principles and theory and then requiring more intense on-the-job training.

Trends like this require the community college president to be engaged in discussions about workforce needs at the community table. These are the conversations that can lead to out-of-the-box strategies to create better results. The relationships that are built open the channels of communication to the point where a business in need will automatically think to reach out to the community college president to help build solutions. We all tend to look for solutions in our circle of familiarity.

K–12 School Districts

- **Strong relationship with high school counselors**—Developing strong relationships with high school counselors, despite that fact that the typical high school counselor reward system is based on how many of their students go to four-year universities.
- **Dual enrollment programs**—Dual enrollment programs are for students taking college classes while still in high school, saving costs of higher university tuition for transferable courses.
- **Sharing facilities**—For example, high school sciences classrooms being used at night or weekends by the college.
- **High school graduation participation**—If the college has certificate or degree programs that high school students complete, the college president could participate in the high school graduation and congratulate those students.

Perspective of a K–12 School Superintendent

Stewart D. Roberson
Superintendent Emeritus, Hanover County Public Schools

The power and the impact of the community college president and school superintendent relationship is truly only limited by the imagination. Both are community thought leaders, and as the faces of public education in the community, they have not only an umbilical relationship, but also a tie/bond/shared interest that affords them the opportunity to advance valuable and transformative educational agendas together.

Both have a stake in promoting the most effective pre-K-to-adult learner continuum and in awarding diplomas, credentials, and degrees that are of the highest quality and value. Both are central players in a locality and region's economic and workforce development efforts.

The president and the superintendent frequently serve the same constituent base; as such, together they experience the glare of the public spotlight and they share the public limelight as the key educational leaders within their county or city. It is only reasonable to expect that collaboration on educational planning and initiatives will occur between the two executives and the entities they lead. It should not be unusual for either or both to lead those collaborative efforts. Efforts should always be made to demonstrate the collaboration publicly.

As both the president and the superintendent may be competing for the same dollars locally (depending upon the state funding structures that can vary nationwide) it is counterproductive for competition between the two to define the relationship. Rather, communities want to see the two executives forming and sustaining a relationship that promotes the common good.

Ideally, the two executives will be comfortable in forming a relationship that includes frequent communication, that makes returning one another's emails or phone calls a priority, that includes outings together, maybe with spouses/partners, and other genuine opportunities to value one another as professionals and humans.

Ideally, the two executives will be entrepreneurial in their quest for one another to experience "wins" for their shared constituencies. They will be alert to opportunities for those wins for both of their organizations, including opportunities to share human resources from within their organization to address and advance shared needs (i.e., academic coaches). Collectively, always, the two executives should be in search of the opportunities to maximize their resources to achieve common goals.

The president and the superintendent must accept that one of their key community roles is to constantly educate the business community about what the two entities are doing to educate the future workforce. Similarly, the two executives should always cast themselves to the business community as being open and caring about the suggestions which can arise about how "human capital" can be engineered to be most productive within workplace settings.

Both executives have a responsibility to lead the academicians within their organizations in a manner that promotes alignment of goals and missions of the two entities, where possible.

The two executives should characterize their professional missions as supporting a continuum of human growth and development. Both should be able to promote the value of investments in pre–K education, for instance, as critical to the return on investment (ROI) increasingly sought by the business community and society. Similarly, both should be able to promote the value of investments in credentials/licenses that are critical to the ROI, and point to the existence of relevant programs that have been developed in collaboration with each of their organizations.

Evidence of well-developed relationships between the president and the superintendent will be readily apparent. Most apparent will be the degree to which their relationship affords them the opportunity to articulate shared values for their organizations and for them, personally. That evidence of their relationship's strength will form the basis for all other opportunities and transformations that follow.

Lastly, the president and the superintendent should be seen in public standing together, extoling one another's value and demonstrating a genuine belief in the power and impact of the relationship between the individuals and their organizations (i.e., graduations, inaugurations, regional committees, Chamber, etc.).

Universities/Other Community Colleges

- **General education transfer programs**—Community colleges should be the greatest feeders of undergraduate students for four-year universities.

- **Co-admissions of two-year and four-year students**—Entrepreneurial community colleges can work with universities to co-enroll students in combined courses.

- **Limited attendance of two-year students in university activities/events**—A helpful recruitment strategy for four-year colleges/universities can be to enable community college students to participate in university events/activities on a limited basis.

- **Reduced in-state tuition rates for border colleges**—Many community colleges located near the state border collaborate with their peers in the neighboring states to allow students to attend each institution at a reduced in-state tuition rate.

Perspective of a Four-Year University President

MICHAEL RAO

President, Virginia Commonwealth University

A strong collaboration between four-year universities and community colleges benefits the students, the communities, and the institutions. Virginia Commonwealth University (VCU) enrolls about 2,000 transfer students each year. Almost all (approximately 1,800) of them come from the Virginia community college system and other Virginia institutions.

In general, they have higher GPA and complete more credits per year than the general student population. They prove to be much more likely to graduate on time. The benefits to the students include reduction in the accumulation of unnecessary credits, which reduces time to degree. In addition, they complete many of their general education credits at lower community college tuition rates while living at home.

The partnerships between four-year universities and community colleges are a vital component in ensuring our institutions achieve our mission to the students and the communities.

Another Perspective of a Four-Year University President

JOHN R. BRODERICK
President, Old Dominion University

There are dozens of tried-and-true measures that have succeeded from Maine to California over the years, so let me try to list some for further consideration:

- Collaboration of faculty across institutions leads to seamless curriculum linkages and financial benefits to students and their families
- Data sharing between both institutions supports transfer experiences and success
- Welcoming admissions and advising personnel on to your campus creates easy navigation for students regarding program inquiry and evaluation of credits, as well as denotes a caring culture
- Offering many onboarding experiences for students strengthens the relationship, especially if some of those are held on your campus
- Help your faculty understand that sharing course outlines and learning outcomes will lead to healthy articulation agreements without course concessions by either institution
- Once agreements are reached, celebrate with public signings and make sure those who did the lion's share of the work receive their due in front of colleagues, students, and media.

My institution, Old Dominion University, has a long and successful marriage with community colleges in Virginia and beyond. Nearly half of our 20,000-plus undergrads attended some level of community college. We are deeply committed to a "reverse transfer" credit practice, encouraging students through direct intervention from advisors to complete their associate degrees. Our approach focuses on these key tenets:

- Putting the student first
- Clear communication between partners
- Simplicity in rules whenever possible

- Collaboration must always win out over competition
- On my campus, people know any answer they require is as close as a phone call or email to our academic and student affairs leadership

Non-Profit Organizations

- **Forgotten partnership potential**—Almost all communities (regardless of size) have multiple non-profits whose purpose it is to make their community a better place to live. Many non-profits have a mission that relates closely to the needs of community college students—including transportation, housing, childcare, and food.
- **Shared space on campus**—Community colleges often have the ability to provide space on campus to serve students (e.g., a non-profit that provides support to people with autism) at a free or reduced cost.
- **Shared communications**—Many non-profits have established networks that can reach many people who have the potential to become community college students. Remember, a high percentage of community college students are first-generation students, and the extra boost from a familiar (and safe) non-profit might be the nudge that results in a person deciding to attend a community college.

Perspective of a Non-Profit CEO

SHERRIE BRACH ARMSTRONG
President/CEO,
The Community Foundation for a Greater Richmond

Creating and sustaining the economic vitality of a local region and community today is more dependent on cross-sector relationships and more public/private partnerships than ever before. Along with the public sector, the nonprofit sector plays a critical role in the delivery of services in areas such as education, human services, workforce development, housing, and arts and culture.

8. Relationships, Relationships, Relationships

The sectors have become more clearly defined as business, public, and nonprofit, and a critical mass of resources is being generated among them and deployed in ways that have an effect on the overall quality of life of a region.

In addition, today's issues are more complex and require a more connected approach to address them, so individuals leading institutions have to be "at the table" and part of the community conversation and the solution.

We have learned while working to solve critical issues in our region that not one sector or institution can do it alone. Success is best achieved when multiple organizations collectively align towards common goals and outcomes.

Specifically, there is crossover between the nonprofits and community colleges/universities in addressing the needs along the cradle-to-career pipeline. A relationship between the college president and nonprofit leaders in those areas is critical due to the roles they play in developing the region's future workforce.

Faith-Based Community

- **Communication fabric of many communities**—One of the least sought out prospects for partnerships are those found throughout the faith-based community in a college's service area. Congregations of all faiths and denominations are generally trusted by residents in a community, and they can be excellent resources for communicating to their members the opportunities available at a college. In addition, many congregations and their members are willing to give to causes like education that help their community. Below are some recommendations from Benjamin Campbell, a senior faith-based leader with some specific and meaningful suggestions:

Perspective of a Faith-Based Leader

THE REV. BENJAMIN CAMPBELL

There is significant opportunity for productive relationships between a community college president and organized communities of faith.

Suggestions on how one might inaugurate and pursue these relationships

- Find a local interpreter: Through conversation with other key personnel or board members, seek one or two persons to whom you might ask about the lay of the land and leadership of the faith communities in your area.
- Invite several leaders to lunch—one or two at a time—and ask them for advice.
- Recognize that faith communities are definitely organized in sub-groups. There is no single "faith community." Therefore, you are seeking to identify some of the major subgroupings and to talk to someone knowledgeable in each of them. This includes both the major religious divisions—Christian, Jewish, Muslim—and the major divisions within each. In addition, in many metropolitan areas, jurisdictional and governmental division are extremely powerful.
- Note that in Christianity the divisions are different from what they were a generation ago. A large number of the congregations catering to persons 40 and younger are "independent" or "non-denominational." "Megachurches" (3,000 members and up) often have little relationship to their nominal denominations. A megachurch with 6,000 or more members should be contacted on its own.

Some of the reasons for making contact with the local faith communities

- Whether these communities represent 15 percent of the local community or 45 percent, they represent the largest identifiable, general groupings of people who can spread and promote the messages of others.
- Traditionally, faith communities have been sponsors and advocates of education and learning. They are in the business of adult education themselves, and are interested not only in the continuing education of their own members, but also in promoting the education and success of other persons in the community.
- Remember that clergy themselves are on the educated end of the population. Most of them have some study beyond a bachelor's degree.

8. Relationships, Relationships, Relationships

- The last point deserves emphasis: If community colleges are in the business of helping people into their first job, or into a better job;—in the business of helping people out of poverty;—in the business of building the equity of the society;—in the business of providing the opportunity for full survivable incomes that will support effective family life;—if community colleges are in this business, some of the greatest potential advocates and supporters for this effort are members and leaders of the faith communities.
- It is important to understand who is in church and who is not. Faith communities do not penetrate the full population as they once did. When dealing with faith leaders it is important to understand whether one is dealing with someone who speaks directly to people associated with their congregation, or whether one is joining in "mission" with that congregation to provide opportunities for others.
- Likewise, it is important to understand that some churches are geographically related to a community and some are not. Knowing this helps one define market and demand.

What are some imaginative partnerships with local faith communities?

- Community colleges have developed partnerships with public school systems and employers. There is no reason that they cannot develop partnerships with faith communities. Courses might be offered at neighborhood churches. They could be religious, or they could be related to employment or human development.
- Faith communities could help develop recruitment and tracks for people at community college.
- Motivated clergy and church leaders can promote particular courses and opportunities in their congregations.
- Development of an incentive program for certain studies or courses promoted by a local congregation. Would the faith community subsidize an offering for certain people? Would it provide transportation?

Tips for dealing with leaders of the faith community

- Note that several Christian denominations are more or less hierarchical and have a central figure who relates to a number of congregations, often in a geographical area larger than the market area of the community college. Roman Catholics and Episcopalians have a bishop of a diocese; United Methodists have a bishop of an Annual Conference, and smaller areas called Districts. Most other denominations have regional groupings of one sort or another. Clergy of independent and nondenominational churches often meet in formal or informal associations. But there are very few well-attended clergy associations meeting regularly and welcoming speakers as there once were.

- I find that local clergy are often responsive when someone in a position of leadership in the community considers them to be important and worthy of contact. If the president of the local community college calls the pastor of a major church and asks him/her to lunch to ask advice and see what cooperation there might be on community issues usually that pastor will gladly respond with interest. The ones who do will be worth making common cause with.
- The least effective thing is generic mailings or e-mails or invitations. A pastor of a congregation is one of the last people in the society whom people think is a communicator to a group of people—so the pastor deals with 50–200 requests to pass on information each week. Clergy are busy people, and even when they are not, they perform "busyness." If I really wanted to contact a clergyman whom I did not know, I would first of all want someone who knew him to contact him. And in any case, I might send a first-class letter and follow it up with a phone call.
- Meet some key people. Ask their advice. Prefer motivation and interest over formal position. Clergy, even in hierarchical denominations, are very independent and are overwhelmed with requests for constructive promotion and intervention. So, the only people who will do something are people who want to, not people who are told to.
- There is a tremendous community of interest between the community college and much of the faith community. It has to do with the building of the community and the edification of our citizens. Get one or two faith leaders into your decision-making body.
- Sometimes there are lay leaders who are experienced and effective at negotiating the strange terrain of the faith communities, and are even effective at contacting clergy. If you find them, adopt them.

The Press and Media—Relationship with Local Media

It is important to recognize that one of the greatest challenges of most community colleges is that the public does not understand the breadth and depth of activities and services offered by the college. The relationship between the college and local media can be a very strong tool to communicate the many activities and successes of a college to the public. The value of "free publicity" can be a great boost to the college budget.

Make sure media contacts know they can contact the college for statements on education and workforce development news in the area. Establish the college as a trusted local higher education expert to the media. If you help them with their job, they will help you with yours.

It is important that the partnership with local media be such that there are regular and frequent stories that help educate the readership about the impact of the college on the community. Contact local media ahead of college announcements such as facilities openings, new curriculum, grants, and similar good news.

Furthermore, over time, there will likely be issues or even crisis that the press will cover. Establishing relationships and trust ahead of that can often be key in ensuring that your college is covered fairly and completely.

Lastly, clearly establish "rules of engagement" with the press. Make sure the staff knows who the college media contacts are at the college. Make sure they know who is authorized to handle inquiries from the press. Remind them at critical times.

Digital and Social Media

The relevance of digital and social media grows every day at a fast pace. Digital content is how much information is consumed and how influence is spread. There are endless ways to share your message. Identify the relevant channels (Facebook, Instagram, Pinterest, Twitter, LinkedIn, etc.) and distribute your content to all of them with a constant, regular pace.

Re-post your news and content across all of the relevant platforms using a social media marketing and management dashboard such as Hootsuite. These tools let you write once and cross post with ease. They let you write content ahead of time and release at regular intervals. They can capture impressions, contacts, shares, and comments. Find out what works and do more of it. Encourage staff, faculty, and students to share posts and contribute comments to grow your audience exponentially.

Finally, publicize your social media results internally. Using your marketing platform for key metrics, produce a regular media report card illustrating results, trends, and the free publicity the school has earned.

Key Chapter Takeaways

- The word "community" in the name of any community college encapsulates the primary focus of the college, with its charge being to make its community a better place to live, work, and play.
- The college president must take the lead in developing partnerships with stakeholders that lead to relationships that will enable the college to better leverage its resources.
- As a new president, you need to engage with the community, but be careful not to overextend or volunteer for committees that don't make good use of time and effort.

CHAPTER 9

A Beggar's Hand or a Vision?
Fundraising and the College

Understanding the Science of Fundraising; a Key Is the Case for Support

Although the primary path of community college presidents has usually been working one's way up through traditional academic ranks, it is no longer uncommon for presidents to develop their careers in student affairs, institutional advancement, finance, or even a career outside academia in the business world.

Regardless of which path is taken to the presidency, it is unlikely that the president has any significant experience in raising money or much knowledge about the science and art of fundraising. That being said, it is important to remember that the greatest golfer of all time had to pick up a club for the first time at some point, just as the greatest opera singer sang the first note even before knowing that a serious study of music was in the future.

Fundraising for community colleges is both an art and a science, and both can be learned. Successful fundraising professionals will attest to the importance of approaching fundraising with a clear and compelling vision, rather than just looking for a handout.

The Compelling Need for Fundraising in Community Colleges

The need is great for community colleges to be successful at raising money outside of the state appropriations and student tuition. In almost all states, state appropriations have not kept up with the cost of doing business, and community colleges have made a concerted effort to keep tuition as low as possible (with tuition rates around the country at about half or a third that of their neighboring four-year colleges and universities). In fact, because enrollments in community colleges have increased over the years and state appropriations have not kept up, in some states the amount of money the colleges receive from the state (in terms of dollars per student) equates to about half of what the college received per student just two decades ago.

A significant challenge unique to community colleges related to fundraising is that of developing and cultivating an alumni base. It is common that students who attend community colleges take the courses they need and move on to four-year universities. Understandably, there are not strong incentives or programs to keep the former students engaged. Furthermore, most community colleges do not have alumni associations or athletics which meaningfully increase the ability for previous students to stay connected.

Four-year universities have been proactively raising money for generations, with many having endowments in the billions of dollars. Most universities also have established traditions with generations of graduates who have been successful in their careers and who are in a position to give back to their alma maters, supported by fond memories of campus life filled with social and academic clubs, football, and the entire menu of exhilarating activities offered throughout their college experience. In addition, universities are better funded by state legislatures and they necessarily have higher tuition than community colleges. In general, four-year universities work hard at raising money and almost all related data reflect greater success at fundraising than by community colleges.

Some might conclude that fundraising for community colleges is imperative to survival during an era of declining enrollments, ongoing decreases in financial support from state legislatures, and declining numbers of high school graduates (thereby greater competition with the four-year universities and proprietary schools for a shrinking pool of prospective students right out of high school).

The College President's Role in Fundraising for a Community College

The college president is the "face of the college" and, in most cases, is the key fundraiser from within the college who must learn to leverage relationships both inside and outside the college to raise money successfully. Although the term "fundraising" is the nomenclature, it is really more about "friend-raising" and educating potential donors about the impact of their community college on their community and region.

College foundation board members can also be major fundraisers, and in the best of all worlds the foundation board members work side-by-side with the college president and chief advancement officer to develop and strengthen relationships with prospective donors and donors.

The President's Relationship with the College's Institutional Advancement/Development Officer

Establishing a strong relationship with the chief development/advancement officer at the college should be a priority. The president will not have time (nor the personal expertise in most cases) to gather the background data about donors and donor prospects and certainly will not be able to manage day-to-day the operational plan nor the staff of the Institutional Advancement Office.

Unless a first-time president has come up through the institutional advancement/fundraising career path (less common for community colleges), it will be likely that the new president has little or no experience in the art and science of fundraising. The good news, however, is that a plethora of seminars and workshops exist to teach both the art and science of fundraising. Some very good ones specifically target presidents and vice presidents of community colleges. The new first-time president should participate in such a seminar as early as possible in his/her presidency.

In addition, if and when a president is in search of a new fundraising professional, one of the criteria should be that the person has a professional credential of Certified Fund Raising Executive (CFRE).

It is imperative that the college president and the chief advancement officer have a very good and trusting relationship as both become the "faces of the college" and they both develop key relationships with community leaders, prospective donors, and donors. Both will share significantly with the various phases of fundraising, including:

1. Identifying prospects and current donors with potential for giving;
2. Qualifying donor prospects to determine whether they might be willing to give to a specific cause;
3. Donor cultivation—hosting and participating in *friend-raising* events.

4. Solicitation—asking the prospect for a donation. Personalize your pitch to your prospects.

5. Stewardship—maintaining a strong connection through recognition and personal engagement. Balance recognition between public recognition and private recognition.

The College Foundation Board

The college president sits on the foundation board, which plays a major role in the ability of a college to raise friends, and therefore, resources (money). For the most part, the foundation board members will not only be significant donors themselves, but their circles of friends, both professional and personal, often compose a major part of the list of those who support and give to the college. In addition, one of the greatest challenges that community colleges still have is that even though the public is aware of and has heard about their local college, the depth of knowledge is usually very shallow. Few people really understand and appreciate the profound impact that the local community college makes on their community.

As is true with all people, foundation board members and prospects have a stronger interest in some things than in others, and those interests vary widely. One person may have a grandchild with autism. Another may be a passionate military veteran. Another may be passionate about keeping the world healthy, having been a nurse earlier in life. The point is that whatever passion prospective donors have, the key to fundraising is to establish a clear connection between the work of the college that intersects with the passions of the prospective donor. Think of foundation board members as ambassadors or as soldiers, or evangelists who have learned enough about their local community college that it has now become one of their passions as well.

From a different perspective, and certainly less important in the grand scheme of things, the College Foundation has much greater flexibility with its raised funds than any other funds (i.e., state appropriations, federal monies, grant monies, and tuition monies) acquired by the college. For instance, the foundation may be able to purchase alcohol (which may be appropriate for certain fundraising events) with money it raised, a use not generally approved for state funds.

Foundation monies can be used to also enhance the salary and benefits of the college president and sometimes other senior officers at the college. However, ensure that any cross use of funds is following financial regulations for your state and your benefactor's expectations.

 Get to Know Your Foundation Board Members
The college president needs to spend time with each foundation board member to get to know them as friends to the college.

It should be remembered that typically only successful people end up serving on foundation boards. They almost always have fascinating and wonderful careers and life histories. It will be very important for the college president to learn about the individual passions and experiences of each foundation board member and understand what passions trigger their willingness to give up their time, energy, and share their treasure to serve on the foundation board.

Many of the foundation board members' reasons for engagement are the same as—or similar to—those of the donors and prospective future donors who will give to the college. Understanding those connections can help leverage the board's effectiveness.

Relationship of the College President with the President/Chair of the Foundation Board

The college president and foundation board president/chair should have a very close working relationship based on trust and respect. After all, both share a passion for the college and both will invest much time and energy in communicating to many people the mission and positive impact of the college on the lives of the students and on the community overall.

The college president and foundation president should meet regularly with the executive director of the foundation to jointly set the foundation board agendas, lead the process of strategic planning, and set long and short-term goals and strategies. And if they really do it right, they will develop the vision and strategies systematically so that the work of the foundation can proceed vibrantly if either the college or foundation president should leave.

Challenge of Working Both Internal and External Relationships to Support Fundraising

The institutional advancement (or development) operation of the college has some unique characteristics that lend themselves to minor challenges. Faculty and staff have a general understanding that the college president raises money, but they don't often understand the process of "friend raising" or "fundraising" as it plays out on a daily basis. It generally takes some investment in the process to raise money, and it is easy for the college president and development officer to focus so much on individuals and organizations outside the college that the faculty and staff can no longer see or understand the fundraising work that they do.

Without going into great detail about the fundraising process itself, colleges often identify an important need at the college, develop a *case for support* to clarify the need and determine how sellable the concept might be to donor prospects, perform a feasibility study with potential donors to test the fundraising waters, and then define an operational plan usually described under the umbrella term "campaign" (whether it be a capital campaign, a scholarship campaign, a major gifts campaign, or something else).

How Does the College President Learn to Master "The Ask?"

In the professional fundraising world, it has been said that the number one reason people do not give money is that they have not been asked. Yet, the thought of asking for money is very frightening and uncomfortable for some people. That being said, although some people have a natural gift to ask for money, others can learn the skill. Although a silly metaphor, there is some veracity in comparing asking for money to that of jumping for the first time from a 10-meter board into the swimming pool—once you get past that initial fear and make the leap, you usually find that the leap was not so scary or painful as originally imagined. With more and more practice, the leap actually gets easier and easier.... Much like making an "Ask" in fundraising.

Continuing a bit more with the 10-meter board metaphor, there can be great benefit to preparing some before actual taking that step. For example, jumping to land feet first, holding your breath while entering the water, and keeping your legs straight until entering the water would be safer techniques than a belly-flop from high up. In fundraising, it is critical to do proper homework about the prospective donor, laying the groundwork of educating and informing the donor about the project (often taking several weeks, months, or even years), and then finding the right time and person to ask. Often the college president should be the one to ask, but not always. Sometimes foundation board member (possibly a CEO who runs in the same social circles as the prospective donor) would be the better person to make the ask, either with or without the college president at their side.

A final comment that would not be a surprise to any experienced president who has successfully fundraised, if the president has done his/her preparation work and homework and cultivated the relationship with the donor over time, there should be no surprise when the time comes to ask a prospective donor for money. Even for a large million-dollar plus ask, it should almost be a formality in process with the donor at that point in time.

Fulfilling Your Benefactor's Dreams

Many people are willing to give small amounts of money for a range of causes, some that they feel strongly and passionately about and others that they believe are "good things" and some support might be helpful. For a larger commitment and gift by a donor, however, the purpose for which funds are being raised is almost always something that the donor is personally passionate about.

Fundraising organizations generally use specialized software and databases that archive information about donors, including their most important priorities for giving, their net worth and capacity to give, and a history of giving (often even having the data for organizations outside of the community college). Almost every community has a small number of the wealthiest in that community who support multiple causes and initiatives and generally are well known for their philanthropy. The case for support should be convincing in providing a donor prospect with a vision of how the world generally—as well as individual lives—would be much better as a result of the initiative for which funds are being raised. In a nutshell, that the college must pursue the raising of friends and money for a *vision*, not a handout.

Donor Cultivation, Stewardship, and Entertainment of Donors

You will encounter complete books written about donor cultivation and stewardship of donors so we will not go into great depth here.

For now, just note that the "art and science of fundraising" is in large part the process of cultivation of relationships between (1) prospective donors and (2) donors who have already given to the college, and who have the potential to "keep on giving."

Often the simple things make the greatest impact on the minds and hearts of donors. A simple but powerful practice that should become a habit is for the college president to send a personal *handwritten* "thank you" note to donors who have contributed above a determined dollar amount to the college. A "thank you" note should go to all donors regardless of the dollar amount from the Office of Institutional Advancement but should come directly from the college president and foundation board member for donors who have a personal relationship with the board member. It is surprising that so many donors never hear a word of any kind from the organization to which they have donated monies. That perceived lack of appreciation can lead to lack of future support.

President's Role in Garnering Appreciation for the Work of the College Foundation and Others

One of the greatest challenges within the culture of the college is that faculty, staff, and students don't often understand the impact that a successful college foundation can have on everything from the facilities and equipment of the college to support for athletics and clubs to student access to the college through scholarships and grants.

There is a need to reinforce communications to faculty, staff, and students about the College Foundation, what it is doing for the future of the college, and a gentle reminder of what it has accomplished in the past. Faculty are busy teaching and they simply may not be exposed personally or directly to the College Foundation, or have not been made aware of the benefits that the foundation provides to the college.

The college president assumes the role of the chief "conveyor" of the good work and positive impact of the foundation on many aspects of the college and student success. Almost all of the college faculty and staff focus internally on their work. on things that directly affect student success; so many, if not most, rarely think about the external relationship that the college has with the community throughout its service area. Certainly, the college president should include significant mention of the work of the foundation in the "State of the College Address," at the annual convocation (or other) event.

9. A Beggar's Hand or a Vision?

The Importance of External Relationships

The area of external relationships is covered in greater depth in Chapter 8. So, it might suffice here to defer to the old adage "out of sight out of mind!" as an ongoing challenge of the college president in truly having faculty and staff both understand and appreciate the work of and impact of the College Foundation. Every college culture is different, but whatever the college culture, the president must communicate effectively and often about the work of the foundation and the impact on student success at the college.

Fundraising in a Small, Rural College

JOHN J. RAINONE
President of Dabney S. Lancaster Community College, Clifton Forge, Virginia

As with any forms of fundraising, "It's all about relationships." This is even more true in rural communities. There is an assumption that it is more difficult to fundraise in rural communities than in urban or suburban settings. There is certainly some truth to this belief. Rural communities have fewer people to ask and fewer corporations and foundations that can provide support than those in urban communities. Thus, large-scale campaigns are more difficult.

However, small and rural colleges serve as the engine in their respective communities by providing key educational opportunities, offering job training, playing a significant role in economic development activities, and supporting small business growth. In many cases, they are the focus of the community. It is not only possible to raise money in rural communities, but it is sometimes possible to raise large amounts of money.

The following strategies are keys to understanding how to be successful with fundraising in rural communities:

1. Understand the need for longer timelines. Expect to have multiple meetings with prospects and use these initial meetings to seek advice and feedback. Many prospects like expressing their

opinions and views and you need to patiently listen, understand, and respect them.

2. Rural residents also place a high value on both loyalty and privacy. Residents tend to be reluctant to publicly share information about others. Individual meetings are more effective than holding group gatherings to share information.

3. Have a large and diverse prospect pool. The typical giving pyramid should include a large number of prospects. A rural community college will need to expand its reach to business and corporate support (typically more effective in urban areas), regional or national foundations, and possibly collaborating with other non-profits to increase exposure and financial support.

4. The college president is key. The president, as the chief advancement officer of the college, must be visible and respected. A key mechanism for developing relations and connecting with external audiences is through presentations to civic organizations, governmental officials, and community forums. Everyone wants to support a successful organization and the community must have faith in the college leader.

5. Provide multiple social interactions. Consider this the "first date." A community college needs to engage people with the mission and the leadership on multiple occasions. Trust is especially important in rural communities. Social networks overlap significantly, and understanding the spheres of influence is critical. It can be very beneficial to have an excuse to meet and mingle in a social setting with no fundraising involved. Special events and house parties, sponsored by board members or prominent volunteers, can be effective.

6. Personalize your approach with everyone. As with any type of fundraising, a personal approach is even more important in a rural community. Never use "Dear Friend" letters. Personalize every invitation, write thank you notes (notes directly from the college President are ideal), and be sure to report to your donors regularly on how their gifts have made a difference, especially in the lives of students.

Community colleges in rural areas are the social engines that drive the community. The college's inclusiveness makes it attractive to potential donors. Fundraising in rural communities is not that much different from any other type of fundraising. "It's all about relationships."

9. A Beggar's Hand or a Vision?

 ## *Key Chapter Takeaways*

- It is imperative to approach fundraising with a clear, compelling vision rather than looking for a handout.
- The college president should get to know the foundation board members and learn about their passions as they relate to the community college mission.
- Fundraising in rural environments can be much more challenging than in urban environments, in great part to the fact that rural environments often have a smaller number of donor prospects and limited local industry.
- The college president should personalize his/her appreciation for the gifts of donors as much and as often as possible.
- The college president should socialize the work and successes of the foundation internally to the college in order to reinforce the importance of community and fundraising efforts.

Chapter 10

Playing Poker with Wild Cards
Government Relations

Government Relations Are Key

Community college presidents and boards must work with government officials and political leaders at multiple levels ranging from national to state and local. Government relationships can neither be ignored nor taken for granted. Although there are some similarities in the relationships with these officials (e.g., the types of information shared and issues addressed) there are also some important differences.

> A few years back, I was on the local college board chair serving six jurisdictions ranging from rural to suburban to urban.
> Our college president asked for a meeting with local officials to work out some critical, time-sensitive funding issues. The jurisdiction at issue had a long-standing reputation of not following through on commitments, making cooperative efforts very difficult.
> I attended the meeting with several of my fellow board members. While the meeting went well, I was a bit annoyed that, despite the publicized agenda, the officials had not prepared for the meeting. However, once briefed, they indicated they understood and would look into the matter. Further, they promised they would get back to us with their decisions.
> They did not. Instead, the meeting and the issues it raised seemed forgotten. I was furious and told the college president not to ask me to rally the board for future meetings with this jurisdiction, as the time would be wasted.
> The president said, "I understand your frustration and your position. However, I do not have the luxury of writing them off. It would not be fair to our students and community, regardless of how frustrating it may be." The president was right.

10. Playing Poker with Wild Cards

At the National Level

The following was contributed by James Lane, Superintendent of Public Instruction at the Virginia Department of Education:

> The federal government has the potential to play a huge role in incentivizing innovation regarding the partnerships between community colleges and P K–12 schools. Numerous grants are available each year to incentivize workforce pipelines; thus, schools and community colleges should partner to apply for these opportunities to leverage extensive resources to create programs to build real-world experience beyond high school.
>
> We have seen that when these types of investments have been made in Virginia, even with state grants or small pilot projects, amazing new opportunities have been afforded to students. A great example of this is CodeRVA in the Richmond metro region. CodeRVA is a partnership involving 13 school divisions and two community colleges to build an equitable workforce pipeline in computer science with a unique approach to instructional delivery. It was born of a small $50,000 state grant which later turned into a $6,000,000 federal magnet schools grant.
>
> The resources at the federal government can take innovations from great ideas to large-scale implementations.

Much of the work of a community college president at the national level involves affiliations with professional associations such as the American Association of Community Colleges (AACC) or the Association of Community College Trustees (ACCT). Membership and active participation in such organizations form a common and more influential voice that can be expressed on an individual basis.

Community college presidents and boards should develop relationships with their representative members of the U.S. Congress. It is important to follow ongoing dynamics often related to funding such as renewal of the Higher Education Act, renewal of Pell Grants, legislation about student loans and student debt (including forgiveness), questions about the quality, cost, and default rates of proprietary schools versus public institutions. For colleges located within a reasonable travel distance to Washington, D.C., it is often worth the time to travel to congressional offices for a visit. Be advised, there is a high risk that the member of Congress will be in committee and the meeting will actually be with a staff assistant, who can be of significant assistance. Building relationships with staff will go a long way toward helping you achieve your goals.

Find ways to invite members of Congress to on-site campus visits when they are back home during breaks. There is nothing more powerful than seeing firsthand the impact of a community college on the lives of the students (and voters), to see the workforce training that takes place to serve local employers, and to see how students can take general education transfer courses at about one-third the cost, maximizing the impact of tax payers' monies. If there is ever an opportunity for a member of Congress to be a graduation speaker, make it happen. That would have multiple benefits that can be long lasting and greatly appealing to the legislator.

At the State Level

States vary on the organization and structures of their state legislative bodies but for the most part there are two primary components similar to U.S. Congress. Most states have something like a House of Delegates and the State Senate. Just as legislators at the national level represent defined legislative districts and yet are responsible for the greater oversight of the entire nation, state legislators have defined legislative districts and are responsible for the well-being of the entire state.

Every community college president should develop relationships with all of the state legislators (both delegates and senators) in the districts that compose their college's service area. These relationships can become very important, mostly in areas of funding, including the general state appropriation to higher education (often assigned per institution or by enrollments) and the other special and capital projects (e.g., a new technology building, funding for a new pilot program with a K–12 school district, etc.). Whenever possible, it can be very helpful to learn about the personal passions and interests of key state legislators. For example, one State Senate Majority Leader happened to be a high school teacher when the legislature was not in session. He was very keen on legislative action (funding and/or policy) that would affect K–12 education in his state. Another key legislator had a granddaughter who had autism, and he connected well with his local community college because the college had a robust support program for community college students with autism. Every legislator has personal special connection and engagement with the community college.

For those who work with legislators (at any level) it is known that within the broader legislative mix, there are key legislators who often dominate and control what will be supported and what will not. In cases where a college service area does not include the key legislators, it is important to find ways to communicate with the influential members. If it isn't possible to develop a relationship with a key legislator whose legislative jurisdiction is outside of the college's service area, then consider developing relationships with legislators who are closest to that key legislator.

Remember that the single greatest challenge with community college funding related to the state legislative process is that many legislators need—and will appreciate being educated about the impact that community colleges make on their region. In addition, very few legislators ever attended a community college as a student, and may have a more natural familiarity with the four-year institutions. So, you may need to educate them and help fill that experiential gap.

The state legislative session deserves additional comment since the funding impact to community colleges reoccurs on a regular basis (mostly on two-year cycles in most states). As state legislators begin to define their funding priorities months before the actual legislative session begins, community college leadership should take the pulse on the hot topics or priorities that are developing for the upcoming legislative session. Whenever possible, colleges should develop strategies that clearly are consistent with the top legislative priorities for the upcoming session. College presidents and government affairs officers should meet with the state legislators before their actual legislative session begins, when life becomes exponentially more chaotic for the legislators.

At the Local Level

Most community colleges receive some type of funding from the local jurisdictions (counties and/or cities) in their service area. Since county/city leadership is local, it would seem that they would strongly support the local community college. That being said, among the greatest challenges of community colleges is the lack of knowledge of or experience by governance officials with their local community college.

In a case in which a community college campus is located in or near the local jurisdiction, it is more likely that the leaders of the locality have some firsthand experience with the community college. The real impact of providing training for residents of the community and a prepared workforce for local employers is much more visible firsthand by local elected officials. Community college leadership and local board members must publicize and share this positive community impact as frequently and poignantly as possible.

It is clearly necessary to develop, nurture, and maintain healthy relationships with the local elected officials who often approve and provide funding for the college—much easier to accomplish when local elected officials are invested in the wellness of the whole of the community and not focused solely on the specific section of the locality where their voters reside. College president can face frustrating complication when the leaders of the local jurisdiction do not work together as a team. For example, it will be more difficult if city council members do not work well with the mayor's office, perhaps resulting in seemingly endless discussion but little decision-making (paralysis analysis). Establishment of funding priorities and the culture of local leadership can fall prey to several competing issues, including area-specific interests and even what appear to be power plays.

Lastly, in community college environments where the colleges are part of a statewide community college system, local elected officials will often contend that "The college is part of the state and therefore the state—not the locality—should pay for and support the college." Yet even in states with statewide community college system state legislatures have cut back on funding for more than two decades. In fact, in Virginia, although the actual number of state dollars provided to the community colleges has gone up over the years, due to increases in student enrollments, the state allotment per student is about half of what it was 20 years ago.

Shared Jurisdictions

Most community college students have a prescribed jurisdictional service area consisting of specific counties, towns, and cities. As a result, relationships are typically formed with the local elected officials for these jurisdictions. Campuses and other facilities are housed within these jurisdictions, and the students live in these jurisdictions. Community colleges often depend on these jurisdictions as a significant source of funding.

Sometimes it can be a bit messy. Students often do not care what your service area is. They may live closer and attend a campus outside of their tax jurisdiction. They may travel outside of their home jurisdiction to take advantage of a curriculum offered nearby. They may live in

10. Playing Poker with Wild Cards

a jurisdiction that is split between community colleges. Because local funding is often based on locality population, student funding could be out of kilter.

Despite this, cooperation for the good of the collective communities is the best course of action. Do not treat your neighboring community colleges as competition. Instead, keep strong, open lines of communication with the neighboring local officials, community college leadership, and K–12 leadership. Find the best ways to serve the students. If funding inequalities need to be addressed, these positive, cooperative relationships will help you find a mutually beneficial solution.

> It is important to find ways to get the local elected officials to understand the positive impact that their local community college makes on the lives of students, their families, and on local employers. One of the best ways to do this is to get local elected officials to walk around the local community college campus and see firsthand the education and training that takes place at the college. It is not enough to have local elected officials attend only occasional meetings on campus where the official walks from their car into a meeting room and then back to their car and away from campus. *Be creative...*

The college leadership (often beyond the president) should have an ongoing information campaign about the positive impact on the local community by the "community's" college.

Regulatory Agencies

For purposes of this section of the book, governmental regulatory agencies include the U.S. Department of Education, your state's Department of Education, the regional accrediting body whose oversight and approval are necessary for students to access federal financial aid, agencies related to construction and OSHA requirements, the Equal Employment Opportunity Commission (EEOC), and others.

Although interaction with these agencies adds value to college leadership it can often feel like added layers of bureaucracy that consumes time and resources with negligible return. This is an area in which The Serenity Prayer can be a most useful tool in managing the interactions with such agencies on a frequent basis. In fact, at large community colleges, there is rarely a week when some agency is not on campus performing an audit of something that often include finances, student files, outcomes, and more. Take heart in the fact that the agencies' goals are to ensure and protect the culture and quality of the student experience.

 ## *Key Chapter Takeaways*

- Generally, state legislators did not attend a community college, and probably neither did family members. We've found that, for the most part, they do not dislike community colleges—they just don't know enough to appreciate them.
- Community college presidents do not have the luxury of "writing off" dysfunctional local government and must find a way to ignite their appreciation for the impact of the local community college on the community.
- Find a way to identify the personal passions of each legislator in the college's service area.
- Make it a point to visit with every state legislator in the college service one-on-one and develop a personal relationship.

Chapter 11

Yin and Yang
Workforce and Economic Development

The Critical Interdependency

If there is a sweet spot in the mission of community colleges, it is the symbiotic relationship between workforce development and economic development. Whether it is a student taking a certificate or degree program in technical training (welding, nursing, computer technician, etc.) or an associate degree to transfer to a four-year university, it all leads to a job and eventually a career. Although one might pose that a transfer degree is not a job, the transfer degree's intended purpose is to lead to a four-year university degree that eventually leads to a job and career. After all, students who graduate from a four-year university don't intend to work as volunteers for the rest of their lives.

When employers are asked about their greatest need to make their business successful, they will most often respond that they need a skilled workforce to meet current and future staffing needs. Meeting this need leads to economic development and the ability of a community to help its local businesses flourish and grow as well as the ability to attract new business or industry to the region. Successful workforce development enables successful economic development: a true yin-yang relationship.

Raison d'être

Why do people go to college? Why do parents send their children to college?

The short answer is to prepare for a career or get a job

Along the way, depending on their path, students mature, grow, build networks, find their path, and are educated. The college experience is an education process—and much more.

Most importantly, colleges (particularly community colleges) are tasked with preparing students to get the job they want and that the community needs.

If you look at economic development activities in a community, you will find several focal points:

- Minimizing the tax burden
- Developing infrastructure
- Readying development sites
- Fostering a high-quality K–12 education system
- Creating a desirable place to live, work and play

In the end, all those efforts can be wasted if that economic development does not focus on ensuring a well-prepared workforce. If the workers are not there, businesses will not grow, come, or invest. That work is primarily on the shoulders of our education systems, with a significant part of that responsibility being the work of our community colleges.

Preparing for a Job Is the Top Priority; There Is No Second Priority

While there is no doubt that colleges and universities are in the workforce development business, much of their curriculum strength and focus are in professions that require four years or more. Community colleges, on the other hand, can prepare a student for a job in a semester, a year, or maybe two years. That "Just-in-Time Teaching" and training means that the entire focus be on providing the education needed to secure and perform well in a job for the foreseeable future. The exception, arguably, might be for students who intend to transfer to a four-year institution to complete their education.

As such, the community college needs to focus on providing education and training that is:

- Purposeful
- Targeted to a job
- Satisfying job entry requirements
- Current and relevant

The test to ensure this is simple. Ask yourself: *when the students successfully complete their programs of study, are they fully qualified for jobs? For what specific jobs are they now prepared?* Ideally, a prospective employer's job description of educational and experiential requirements should *match the objectives of your curriculum.*

Connecting with Local Economic Development Groups

Increasing competition for new and expanding businesses makes economic development crucial to the financial vibrancy and stability of localities. Many organizations and resources support economic development though site readiness and infrastructure improvements, tourism investments, incentives and tax abatements, grants, and direct development of entertainment venues and other economic drivers. The many organizations that are part of any community's economic development efforts can go well beyond local economic development offices.

Many communities have regional economic development promotion offices whose mission is to brand the region by highlighting its competitive benefits and features. A key part of the messaging includes workforce readiness. Obtaining a seat on the board can help ensure that your community college is ready for the needs of any newly arriving businesses, and that the workforce readiness and a nimble community college training system stays in the forefront of the regional marketing campaigns.

Connect with local work incentive programs and organizations, many of whom focus on serving the economically disadvantaged, career changers, the mentally or physically challenged, or veterans. Typically, these organizations work with their constituents to promote educational opportunities, manage grants and other funding resources, and track progress as they work to improve lives. Your community college is often the best local provider of the education from which many of these citizens could benefit.

Economic Development Metrics

Among the many lessons from Peter Drucker, this is probably the most useful:
"If you can't measure it, you can't improve it."

Let's say you have heard that your community college takes too long to adapt your curriculum to emerging workforce development needs. The local businesses have indicated that this is stifling economic development, investment, and expansions. What to do? Your community college develops a strategy to shorten the time-to-market for new workforce training offerings with greater input from industry and professional practitioners. Soon, the staff and faculty get behind the push, and the local businesses are excited about the potential. A year into the efforts, you are again meeting with the business community and they ask the question: "So, how much have you been able to improve on this effort?"

A verbal acknowledgment that you are "working hard" or "dedicated" to the improvements will fall on deaf ears. Instead, identify and track just a few key performance indicators (KPIs) to measure progress. For Just-in-Time Teaching, that might include:

- Number of new certificates or licensures issued in last year
- Number of students enrolled in classes that are less than a year old
- Number of new custom contract classes/enrollment for local businesses

Tracking these KPIs (over years) will provide hard proof of your efforts and strategy. It will also identify when those strategies need refinement. Finally, it is a tangible representation of your efforts to meet workforce development needs.

> You have likely heard of SMARTY goals (specific, measurable, attainable, relevant, time based, and yours). When developing tactics to meet community workforce development needs, define all of them in SMARTY terms. The measures in the goals (M) become your KPIs.

One Student and One Job at a Time

In spite of the fine efforts of higher education career counselors, many higher education institutions tend to look at their graduates as a *group*, "the new workforce." Upon graduation, students are released onto the workforce. With a little bit of luck, our capitalist meritocracy will sort out the right fit for the jobs at the right pay. From a national or regional perspective, it would seem that that is what is happening. However, companies do not hire *workforces*; they hire *workers*. And graduates need jobs.

If your community college has properly prepared its graduates for specific jobs or careers, the real test is first securing the jobs, and then long-term success in those jobs. The focus of community college career placement support should be narrow: get the student in front of local employers so they can get jobs. That is best done one student at a time.

> Most students are not fully prepared to find and land a job. Your college can do much to help them succeed. They likely need assistance and guidance with job market research, networking, resume preparation, references, application support, interview support, and follow-up strategies. Make job placement assistance a true college priority. Set hire targets. Celebrate each win.

Public Classes

Community colleges can offer workforce development programs in different ways. A common way is to offer up a selection of regularly scheduled public classes that are advertised to prospective students and their employers via printed and online catalogs, flyers, and email blasts. As a rule, these classes seek to achieve specific competencies, skills, certifications, or general workforce critical/soft skills. Often, these classes are taught as a series (e.g., Project Management 1, Project Management 2).

Common examples are:

- Microsoft Office Applications
- Programming Languages
- Project Management
- IT Security
- Geo-Spatial Fundamentals
- Basics in Trades (Electrical Theory, Gardening Basics)
- Customer Service, Conflict Management

Often, prospective students already have jobs. Offering classes after hours or on weekends might be the best way to reach these students. If you can offer two sessions, can you let the students make up classes in other sections when work or life gets in the way of attendance?

Employers often will pay the cost of training for their employees your students! Your business office should make that process as easy as possible. Meet with local employers to collaborate with them to meet the training needs of the employer and the students. Ask them:

- Can you invoice the employer directly? That way you can remove a barrier for the student that might have trouble paying up front.
- Can you offer a guarantee? If the student does not pass the certificate exam, they can retake the class.
- Can you facilitate the exam onsite? Sending the students elsewhere to take the exam consumes time and complicates the process.

Finally, attendance in these classes should be monitored closely. Ensure that the classes are relevant and up-to-date, best accomplished by having an ongoing conversation with industry and professional experts and advisory groups, asking for—and heeding—their input related to the quality of the training.

Try to ensure the design of technical classes around industry standards or certifications. Beyond exposure to the material, ideally the student would earn an industry-recognized certificate. This focus prepares the student for a job they were previously unqualified for and helps the prospective employer recognize their readiness. Many such courses culminate in proctored exams that can earn the students a certificate.

Just-in-Time Teaching, Credentials, and Licenses

MARY ELIZABETH CREAMER
Vice President of Workforce Development and Credential Attainment, Reynolds Community College/ Brightpoint Community College

The Virginia Community College System (VCCS) began its Fast-Forward workforce development-training program in 2016. At the time, half of the job openings in Virginia required some post-high school education, but not a bachelor's degree.

11. Yin and Yang

FastForward was designed to train the Virginia workforce for these jobs through technical education and relevant certifications. The promise was that many in the Virginia high school educated workforce could become qualified for better paying, more fulfilling jobs.

Since 2016, more than 16,000 credentials have been earned in logistics and transportation, healthcare, welding and manufacturing, skilled trades, information technology, customer service, and education. Classes are typically six to 12 weeks and are designed so students can still work and keep their current jobs. Many of the credentials are stackable (complementary), opening up even more opportunities. Costs for the classes vary (around $3,000), with tuition assistance availability for those in need.

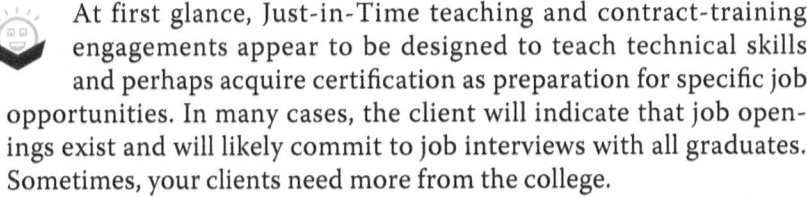 At first glance, Just-in-Time teaching and contract-training engagements appear to be designed to teach technical skills and perhaps acquire certification as preparation for specific job opportunities. In many cases, the client will indicate that job openings exist and will likely commit to job interviews with all graduates. Sometimes, your clients need more from the college.

For instance, in one case for Commercial Driver's License (truck driver) training, the prospective employer asked that the classes be structured with long 8-hour days. The hope was that students that could not handle that long a day, as they would on the job, would self-eliminate.

Similarly, another client company asked that the class be scheduled very early in the morning to determine whether the students would show up to class, as they would have to at work.

Community college workforce development class is often the beginning of the job interview.

Workforce Development

THEODORE RASPILLER
President, Brightpoint Community College

The litmus test for today's community colleges is this: "How well are you performing relative to local workforce needs?" Period.

Much of traditional technical and trades training will increasingly need to morph into more advanced skills training as today's manufacturing and building trades become more sophisticated and automated. This will be very expensive. For it to work, it will require partnerships with local employers to bridge the cost and expertise of teaching to meet the needs of an increasingly skilled workforce.

A key component for today's "nontraditional students" and workforce is stackable credentials. These lifelong learners need to keep their current jobs, learn skills, and earn credentials. Then they can move to a high paying job. Rinse and repeat.

The community college (unlike a four-year college) has many "off ramps" for their students. Most are opportunities in new jobs and specialties, opened because of training, licenses, and credentials. It includes ramps to four-year colleges and universities, saving money and prequalifying students that might have otherwise struggled with admission.

Despite much higher costs, competition between for-profit colleges and community colleges continues to be tough because of marketing campaigns that promise a job. On top of that, many for-profit colleges target populations that qualify for significant financial aid. That can be very compelling to well-meaning parents. Oftentimes, the cost differential is irrelevant or simply unknown to the consumers.

Internships and informal apprenticeships solve several problems:

- It is tough to attract qualified instructors familiar with the latest in their specialties. Many are priced out of our market. However, if our students can get on-the-job training at their facilities, that gap can be bridged with minimal college resources.
- Internships and apprenticeships provide an on-ramp for the jobs the students are seeking. Oftentimes, your students can skip an onerous recruitment and selection process.
- The local experts at these employers can be invaluable in maintaining relevance and currency for curriculum advisory boards.
- Equipping our community colleges with the latest tech is expensive. Leveraging our local businesses equipment for an intern or apprentice makes the training affordable and accessible.

Dr. Stephen Moret discusses the emerging dominance of talent-driven economic development in "Setting the stage for talent-driven economic development" (brookings.edu).

11. Yin and Yang

Economic Development

Stephen Moret
*President and CEO,
Virginia Economic Development Partnership*

Talent-driven economic development is the future (and largely the present) of effective economic development efforts.

There is ample evidence that talent considerations have come to dominate the site-selection criteria of traded-sector firms as they choose where to place job-creating business investments.

A fundamental challenge is that public and private funders of [Economic Development Organizations] still largely evaluate their effectiveness using short-term measures of success—principally, the amount of new jobs and capital investment associated with project announcements. This emphasis often runs counter to a focus on talent-driven economic development.

For most [Economic Development Organizations]—in particular, those serving a locality or region—talent-driven economic development will mean proactive engagement in generating insights on gaps between talent supply and demand, facilitation of connections between employers and educators, and advocacy for policy or programmatic initiatives associated with talent development, deployment, or attraction.

 Key Chapter Takeaways

- Recognize that successful economic development depends significantly on successful workforce development.
- Curriculum outcomes should match job skills and knowledge required for employment.
- For workforce development initiatives, identify a few KPIs to help illustrate your progress and effectiveness in developing and delivering on the community's needs.
- Make job placement assistance a true college priority. Set hire targets. Celebrate each win.

Chapter 12

An Achilles Heel or Seven Deadly Sins

Vulnerabilities That Can Put a College Presidency at Risk

In Greek mythology, when Achilles was a baby, it was foretold that he would die young.

To prevent his death, his mother Thetis took Achilles to the River Styx, which was supposed to offer powers of invulnerability, and dipped his body into the water. However, as Thetis held Achilles by the heel, his heel was not washed over by the water of the magical river.

Achilles grew up to be a man of war who survived many great battles. In the myths surrounding the war, Achilles was said to have died from a wound to his exposed heel, which was the result of an arrow—possibly poisoned—shot by Paris.

Presidential vulnerabilities are similar to the Achilles heel. They come in two sorts: those that are like tsunamis, with little notice of their arrival yet full of devastating force and negative energy with potential for great destruction; and those that are more like cancers, growing over time and eroding the good health of the presidency and/or the institution.

Let us look at some of the most common areas of presidential vulnerability.

Dangers of Presidential Ego Inflation

The "presidency" is much grander than the person who is "president." The college president should never forget this. Although college presidents were awarded attention throughout their successful climb to the presidency, the attention bestowed upon them as president is probably exponentially greater than any they have experienced before. This constant attention must be managed very consciously and deliberately to enable the president to succeed. The president must be cognizant of and attentive to the perceptions of his/her ego. An over-inflated ego is distasteful to most people and it can not only result in burnt bridges in relationships, it can prevent such bridges from ever even being built. There is no reason not to be humble.

Lack of Clear Institutional Values

The college president is the person who is in the best position to represent, clarify, and reinforce institutional values. When things get complicated and pressures mount for the president to do something other than "the right thing," it is the personal and institutional values that will serve as a beacon to guide the president (and therefore the rest of the college) ultimately to do the right thing. When the president finds him/herself in a complex situation, others will be watching the president, hoping for proper and fair action. The action taken by the president will most likely either strengthen or weaken the presidency and their ability to lead and influence in the future.

Weak Financial Management of the College

Monitoring and managing the finances of their college is critical to the success of the college and the president. Although checks and balances exist for almost all institutions, it is possible in today's world of online banking and electronic transferring to misdirect funds or spend funds in ways outside of legal guidelines. These missteps can result in funds either disappearing or the federal/state government determining that funds were misspent and, therefore, must be returned, often with a steep financial penalty.

In addition, the complexities of federal financial aid require the oversight of experienced professionals who understand the eligibility requirements and who can work with the bureaucracy of federal and state agencies.

Weak or Dysfunctional Leadership Team

The old adage "a chain is only as strong as its weakest link" offers a lot of wisdom to a community college president. One of the most important responsibilities of college presidents is to surround themselves with the best team possible. The president should build a team of professionals who have greater strengths and expertise in their specific areas of operation than the president.

The president should dispatch those talented individuals to perform the work of the many differing operations of a college. Micromanagement is not an option; it limits the scope of effectiveness of the operation and diminishes employee morale.

It has been said that:

> A successful leader who works in isolation can only influence that which they can personally get their arms around. However, the leader can significantly expand the sphere of influence by holding hands with others.

There is much truth to this concept. Successful college presidents do not have time to micromanage nor engage in a great level of detail in college operations. Therefore, they need a strong, trustworthy, and skilled leadership team.

Recognizing the value of diversity also can and should be a key strength that leads to presidential success. One of the worst things a college president can do is hire others who look like, think like, and are essentially clones of the president. That being said, however, it is imperative that members of the diverse team share the fundamental values that lead to right and wrong decisions and shape the culture of the institution.

Lack of Political Savvy

Jeffrey J. Kraus
Assistant Vice Chancellor for Strategic Communications,
Virginia Community College System

Successful community college presidents need to understand the dynamics and influence of politics and as much is possible. They should lead their college in a non-partisan way. The ebb and flow of political parties (and their elected politicians) is in a state of constant change and, for obvious reasons, the college president does not want to be perceived as pro-one-party and anti-the-other-party.

In addition, one of the most important roles of presidents is to raise funds for their colleges. Donors come in all shapes and sizes, including a full range of political loyalists from the extremely conservative to the extremely liberal and everything in the middle.

It is critical that the college president never lose sight of the most important common denominator of improving the quality of life for the students, their families, and the employers throughout the college service area. The common denominator, of course, is to provide students with a strong education (both in technical areas and life skills) and the local employers with a skilled workforce.

Hiring a New Dean: The Art of Saving Face

By far the most complex and time-consuming challenges are those related to human resources and the hiring of talented people with the right combination of personal values, education, training, and experience. Below is a real scenario that played out with a mix of politics, HR policy, good ethics, the "right thing to do," and more…

As college president, I believed so strongly that the most important decision that I or the college would ever make was who to hire. We would only be as good as our talented team members and "bench depth." I believed this strongly enough that I took the time to interview the finalist for every full-time position at the college, including every position from the executive vice president and deans to teaching faculty, grounds workers, and custodial staff. Although booked as an interview, it was really more of a fireside chat with the president during which the applicant shared his/her life story with me, talked about why he/she wanted to be part of our college, and concluded by discussing the college mission, the importance of customer service, and the culture that we aspired to strengthen at the institution.

In this particular situation one of the deans' positions was open at the college and the search committee had gone through its regular process of paper screening, interviewing a small number of candidates, and then recommending their top choice for my presidential interview and hopefully, final approval to hire the individual.

The candidate recommended was someone who already worked at our college in a lower level position. He was someone who generally liked to stay under the radar, not doing anything spectacular in his work but also avoiding anything that might lead to confrontation. In other words, he was a middle-of-the-road performer who was pleasant and well liked but not particularly respected for top notch work. The teaching faculty on the search committee wanted him because they knew he would maintain "same-old same-old" and not rock the boat or increase faculty workload by initiating new ideas or changing anything. He had a proven record of being a mediocre performer who would not take either the dean's position or the academic school to a higher level of performance.

So between the proverbial "rock and a hard place" are (1) appease the faculty on the search committee and hire him, knowing that it would not be in the long-term best interest of the college nor the students or (2), not hire him and create a situation in which faculty would be upset with some even attempting to sabotage the new dean's success since they were not the person's top choice. The obvious choices did not appear to include a winning option.

But here is how it played out.... My scheduled interview with him was on a Wednesday. I went through the regular interview/fireside chat process and concluded that he simply would not provide the leadership that I needed. After he left my office, I called the academic vice president and asked her to come to speak with me. I informed her that hiring the in-house candidate in this case would not be in the best interest of the college and that I would not do so.

However, it was Wednesday. I asked the academic vice president to meet with him the next day in a private setting and inform him that the president had decided not to hire him as the new dean and, that the decision of whom to hire would not be made until the following Monday. He had a couple of options. One would be to continue as a candidate, knowing that he would not get the position and that someday he might be interviewed for a position somewhere and the question could be asked "didn't you apply for a dean's position at your own college and not get the position? What happened there?" The other option might be that he withdraws from contention before Monday, when the president would formally make and announce the hiring decision.

He chose to withdraw as a candidate for the position on Friday. As president, I never had to engage in a conversation with faculty about why he wasn't hired at their recommendation and, it saved face for the in-house candidate. And even more importantly, I was able to "do the right thing" on behalf of the students and the college overall. Whenever possible, always save face for others!

12. An Achilles Heel or Seven Deadly Sins

Misbehavior in the Presidential Fishbowl: Disrespectful Behavior, Sexual Harassment and Bullying

Leadership at its core, and especially for the president, does not allow for disrespectful behavior, including a wide range of actions from sexual harassment and bullying to discrimination by race, gender, sexual preference, and so on. The college president should be the role model both inside and outside the college for all faculty and staff, as well as for the community as a whole.

In addition, the mystique of the presidency results in many people having their eyes on college presidents, constantly observing what they do.

> One university president in recent years was stopped while driving in his community and given a DUI.
>
> The very next week the same president was stopped in a neighboring state and received another DUI. All of this became public.
>
> As one might expect, that individual did not last long in the presidency and was fired by his board, and the whole process was a major embarrassment for the college and community.

Seven Deadly Sins

John A. Manzari
College Board Member, Reynolds Community College, Virginia
College Board Member/Chair, Broome Community College, New York

Although the seven deadly sins (pride, wrath, lust, greed, sloth, envy, and gluttony) usually imply a religious message, all seven of them are applicable to the presidency if recognized in presidential behavior. Here are some examples of how the president's activities may go astray...

Pride: Almost every activity that results in a significant success on the campus is a team effort. Whether it is with the faculty, board, or other groups, the president should share the success with all involved. The president is the captain of the team, not the only player.

Wrath: No one likes to see uncontrolled feelings of anger or rage. If corrective action is required, it should be done with as much privacy as possible. Will Rogers wisely observed, "People who fly into a rage always make a bad landing."

Lust: Our current society is much more accepting than it has been in the past; however, lust is the downfall of many individuals in high positions. This includes not only the presidents of colleges, but also presidents of countries.

Greed: Presidential greed should be avoided. Taking advantage of the situation for personal gain when not contractually sound may be grounds for termination.

Sloth: A consistent impression of the president not having interest in college activities, or being lazy or generally disinclined can spell disaster. In fact, one could argue that it would be rare for this deadly sin to exist, as it would have destroyed their career before the individual ever made it to the college presidency.

Envy: Envy is the desire for others' traits, status, abilities, or situation, and at a minimum can distract the college president from the focus on critical tasks.

Gluttony: Gluttony is an inordinate desire to consume more than that which one requires. Community colleges seem to be constantly asked to "Do more with less." The wise use of resources is highly important to the success of a college.

Key Chapter Takeaways

- The "presidency" is much grander than the person who is the president. Failure to understand that distinction will likely lead to a dangerously inflated ego.
- We all have weaknesses—our Achilles heel. Assessing weaknesses and then surrounding yourself with those who can compensate is a key to building an effective leadership team.
- Lead with values: The college president cannot be a part of all decisions. Clear and shared institutional values are essential to consistent and proper leadership.
- The college president is in a very public position. Missteps will likely be discovered and viewed harshly.

Chapter 13

Walking the High Wire

Balancing Work and Play

Personal Health and Fitness

There is a reason why just before takeoff the flight attendant announces that in an emergency, oxygen masks will drop and it is important for you to put your own mask on first, before helping others with theirs.

If you cannot breathe, you cannot help

That same principle applies to the community college presidency concerning good health. Serving the needs of others and active leadership will suffer if the president becomes physically unhealthy.

The demands of a community college presidency can be heavy in time, energy, and pressure. The president must be healthy and strong in order to carry out his/her duties with the greatest possible success. A routine of healthful eating and exercise should be among the top priorities of any president. It is also a good way to lead by example.

Regular medical checkups and a regimen of exercise multiple times per week are necessary for any president to maintain a high level of good health. Some presidential contracts contain language requiring the college president to undertake a complete physical exam on an annual basis. This is evidence that college boards and community college systems view good health as a top priority for their president.

Balance of Work and Play

The dynamic of balancing work and play can be one of the greatest challenges for those striving to build a career. Once a president has begun to engage the community, the opportunities to participate on local board and leadership groups begins to escalate.

Chambers of Commerce, Rotary Clubs, and a host of others will hold early morning breakfast meetings, most on a weekly or monthly basis. Then, after a long day, other groups may meet for dinner or drinks. There frequently are days when back-to-back meetings are held throughout the entire day, leaving the college president with little time to pause, eat lunch, or take a breather. It can be easy for a college president to gain weight due to a combination of a lack of physical exercise and finding themselves in frequent lunch meetings, during which the food provided is often convenient to the host but is not necessarily based upon a manageable well-intended diet.

College presidents can frequently be heard telling their staff that the "Number one priority is family!" They encourage colleagues to take the necessary time off to attend to an aging parent, a sick child, or other family need—yet they often find it difficult to practice that prioritization themselves.

Vacation Time for the President and All Staff at the College

One of the ways college presidents can help with the balance of work and play is by using earned vacation time. Everyone needs to get away from the pressures of the job periodically. Community college presidents should speak loudly and clearly with staff throughout the college that vacation time is an earned benefit. Faculty and staff should not feel guilty because they choose to get away from work and relax for a few days. While everyone understands that vacation time is officially described in print in human resource policy manuals, the culture of an institution can often steer employees away from the actual benefits policy to one in which people are discouraged to take time away from work. Reality is that the workload simply never seems to end.

In a department unit with numerous employees, vacation time should be coordinated to avoid having everyone taking leave at the same time. Americans often think of summer as the time of year when vacations are typically held. School is out for K–12 students and it is a popular time to go to the beach, or the mountains, or simply stay at home and

13. Walking the High Wire

enjoy just being away from work. There is a visible cadence to college operations, however, and some operational areas are typically under greater pressure in a seasonal mode (i.e., admissions staff are extremely busy during the weeks just before a semester start).

Finally, the president needs to "walk the talk" and take time off.

Importance of a World-Class Executive Assistant

It may seem at first odd to place the role of the president's executive assistant in the chapter about "Balancing Work and Play," but from a practical perspective, the executive assistant will be extremely proficient in encouraging, reminding, and helping the college president maintain a healthier sense of life balance.

The executive assistant typically is the air traffic controller of the college president's schedule. The executive assistant can help the president by planning ahead and building the president's schedule around a block of time that enables the president to take a week or two off from work. In some cases, it works well for the executive assistant to schedule his/her vacation during the same time as the college president, so that there is no break in the actual day-to-day support for the president. In other cases, the executive assistant tries to use vacation time that differs from the president in order to maintain a voice of continuity in the college president's office.

The executive assistant can help with the president's health balance, by inserting breaks in the schedule of meetings, and can influence and minimize the chaos of an overbooked day.

> NOODLE MANAGEMENT—We sometimes hear the phrase "There are too many noodles on our plate!" This is a metaphor for having too many things to do, too many tasks and responsibilities, and simply too much work. For decades (even at lower levels throughout my career), I have been in discussions about "noodle management." The intention of the person leading the conversation is to reduce the number of "noodles" for which each person who is accountable. However, without exception, the outcome has always been to simply get a larger plate!
>
> Find agreement about what will not be done (prioritize) and remove some items from the plates!

Role of the President's Spouse

Nam Rhodes

*President's Spouse,
J. Sargeant Reynolds Community College*

The role of and engagement of a community college president's spouse can be as varied as the imagination will allow. There are key events throughout the year which the spouse of the president usually attends, and although they do not play an official role, they often serve to greet and welcome guests as if they were an ambassador for the college. In fact, many people enjoy meeting the spouse of the president, as it provides an opportunity for a peek inside that presidential mystique that comes with the job.

Entertaining is also an area where the president's spouse can play a significant role. It might simply be hors d'oeuvres, or dinner in the president's home, or playing the role of gracious hostess/host at a local restaurant. One president's wife loved to entertain in her home, was a hobby chef, and kept the home always ready for an impromptu gathering of guests that might include board members, donors/donor prospects, students, and even faculty and staff. In this case, the experience was considered to be a "value-added" opportunity for the president and spouse. In another case, a president's spouse felt that such openness to the president's home was an intrusion and encroachment on personal space and avoided any events on the home front as much as possible. The range of interest on the part of the president's spouse to use their home as a venue for entertainment ranges from one extreme to the other and includes every possibility in between.

Regarding entertainment of board members, donors/donor prospects, local elected-officials, and other guests, it is most common for the spouse to engage in activities that occur in a nice restaurant or in facilities on the college campus. After all, a good ambassador knows that positive engagement on the college campus can be much more powerful than the same type of engagement at a restaurant or neutral venue. In cases where the college has a culinary arts program there can be an added benefit if the program faculty and students cater the event, demonstrating their learning and the value of the program to the community.

The types of entertainment can vary tremendously. One college president was married to another former college president, and they created a tradition of having a pizza party at their home every Friday evening. They invited two or three different couples over every Friday for a relaxed "end-of-week" casual wind-down of pizza, beer, and wine.

Another presidential couple lived on a 40-acre lake about 30 minutes out of town, and would invite one or two other couples over for a grill out with pontoon boat riding or kayaking during the weather-comfortable months. This would often result in sitting around a campfire singing songs or telling stories. The memorable twist was that the experience brought back nostalgic memories of camping in the woods in their youth for attendees.

The role of the spouse needs to be understood and agreed upon to maximize the effectiveness without straining the relationship.

Key Chapter Takeaways

- Above all things, the health of the college president is most important. Make this a top priority—eat healthily, exercise routinely, and invest time in *both* work and play.
- Lead by example and take your vacation time, strongly encouraging staff and faculty to do the same.
- Hire a world-class executive assistant who can manage the details hour-by-hour and encourage (and help design) a balanced schedule.
- Find the most effective niche for the spouse to support the president and the college if at all possible. In most cases, spousal engagement can enrich the relationships between the president and others. It also helps the spouse get a glimpse of the complex role of and demands on the college president, which could even help in their relationship.

Chapter 14

A Solemn Duty

*Hiring, Evaluating and
Removing the President*

As is likely now clear, there are many ways to govern a community college. In some cases, the college board is an appointed advisory body. In other systems, college board members are elected and have a significant governing role and taxing authority. Some college boards may get involved in the president's performance evaluation process, or in terminating the president's service, or they may get involved in selecting a replacement. In all likelihood, college boards have roles and responsibilities for all of these.

In fact, it is likely that the president's employment is the only individual personnel matter in which a board has direct involvement

The Board's Role and Responsibilities in Presidential Oversight

Board responsibilities regarding presidential performance evaluations vary greatly. In some cases, there is no local board involvement; in others, the board has full responsibility for this function. Regardless of the job, a regularly scheduled, well-defined performance evaluation, consisting of accountability with qualitative and quantitative measures, should play a critical role in ensuring high performance and success of the president.

The primary goal of any executive's evaluation is to maximize the performance of the organization through the executive's leadership and action. Regardless of the evaluation responsibilities of the board, there are key components that make the process effective:

14. A Solemn Duty

- Clear and defined evaluation processes and policy;
- Regular evaluation schedule;
- Clear board member understanding of the role and responsibilities of the office of the president;
- Understanding the institution's strategic plan and tactical implementations;
- Progress review process that includes goals, activities, and tasks against qualitative and quantitative measures.

Regularly scheduled formal presidential evaluations provide a baseline for future performance comparisons, both positive and negative. Using a performance evaluation to address a specific, current concern or issue is typically more punitive than useful to the college or the president.

Instead, if a regularly scheduled review process is in place, the focus can be on growth and improvement of the organization and the executive.

Everyone's performance is subject to ebbs and flows over time. A regularly scheduled performance evaluation process is an effective way to manage performance over time.

In all cases, specific, clear, and measurable goals are fundamental to an effective and meaningful presidential evaluation process.

Evaluation Criteria

The purpose of periodic performance evaluations is to:

- determine (after the fact) how the person has met the periodic objectives;
- assess key competencies and skills and identify opportunities to improve performance;
- determine expectations for the next review (goals, accomplishments, and activities);
- clarify any needs from the organization to help support future success.

Expectations for each must be set in advance of the evaluation so that the president can measure and adjust throughout the year in order to optimize results.

Setting Measurable Goals

In some cases, measurable goals are set outside the college by state or federal authorities. In others, a more autonomous board may set them. Typical metrics include:

- Enrollment measures
- Graduation and completion rates
- Transfer rates
- Credentials awarded
- Budget performance measures
- Diversity measures
- Accreditation compliance measures
- Personnel turnover
- Faculty/staff relationships
- Fundraising accomplishments
- Community engagement measures

Because these outcomes can be objectively measured and compared against peers, they represent the easiest component of the evaluation. Typically, once goals are set, they are reported to the board a few times during the year, with a final review during the annual summary review of the performance evaluation. Key metrics should be easily understood, easily measured, and relevant. Annual goals for the metrics should be true challenges, yet achievable.

It is not enough simply to state the goal. An agreed-upon strategy should be in place. A measured goal statement would look a little like this:

Goal

The graduation rate for full time students will increase from 34 percent to 38 percent by January.

Limits

Strategies that dilute the quality of the education or redefine graduation are not to be employed to achieve this goal.

Strategies

- *Early warning alerts for potential dropouts will be implemented, followed by student counseling.*
- *All non-graduates lacking six or fewer credits will receive a follow-up phone call from student services before the semester add/drop date.*

No Surprises

The college board and the president are best served by adhering to the defined purpose of the evaluation:

To improve the performance of the college and the president through periodic evaluations of both.

The presidential evaluation process should not be a "gotcha" process. It should be a process that both the college board and the president agree is meaningful, fair, and consistent. Each year, before the evaluation begins, the college board should meet with the president, review the process, and determine whether anything needs to be adjusted. Such collaborative planning reinforces the likelihood of matching ultimate goal expectations.

Effective Evaluation Practices

A comprehensive evaluation process ideally comprises three inputs:

- Performance against goals
- Competencies
- Constituency/stakeholder input

Performance Against Goals

Measuring performance against goals is done by simply listing each of the president's *SMARTY* goals along with its current objective status (complete or not, measure, growth). A short narrative providing insight into the criteria is a plus, as is graphical progress indicator to scan for areas of success as well as others that need attention. Lastly, details into the metrics should be provided as an attachment or link to support a deeper dive if needed.

Goal	Target Measure	Current Results
Increase earned certificates	20% increase from last year	22% increase as of May 20 ⬆
	Most of this increase is due to the opening of the CDL School.	

Competencies

Skillful leadership of any large, complex, organization requires critical competencies, and everyone has a different mix of strengths and weaknesses. Detailing and assessing these critical skills and competencies prove a useful tool the regular evaluation, when the college board can assess the president across them. In some cases, the president will have mastered these, in others, the process may reveal a professional development opportunity.

Competencies	Outstanding	Exceeds	Satisfactory	Development Opportunity	No input on this
Leadership and Supervision					
Fosters a collegial environment	✘				
Motivates and develops	✘				
Promotes a positive culture	✘				
Builds and leads effective teams	✘				
Delegates effectively	✘				
Treats others with respect	✘				
Recruits outstanding talent	✘				
Effectively manages diversity	✘				
Fosters ethical and accountable behaviors	✘				
Plans for the future	✘				
Communications					
Communicates openly and clearly	✘				
Articulates visions, concepts and ideas	✘				
Effectively promotes the college	✘				
Encourages feedback	✘				
Business/Financial					
Develops and shapes strategies	✘				
Effectively manages financial and material resources		✘			
Effectively raises funds	✘				
Balances short and long term priorities	✘				
Supports appropriate level of technology			✘		
Organization					
Effectively establishes priorities	✘				
Effectively analyzes information and data	✘				
Identifies and solves problems	✘				
Generates and pursues new ideas	✘				
Handles multiple demands effectively	✘				

14. A Solemn Duty

Constituency Input

The president has to deal with multiple constituency groups. These groups and their leaders have concerns and needs that require the attention of the president. These groups manage and represent the organizations and resources of the college needed to fulfill its mission and often include:

- Teaching faculty (Faculty Senate)
- Professional staff (deans, department heads, administrative management)
- Classified support staff (Classified Council)
- College board
- Foundation board
- Senior management (cabinet, CEO direct reports)

Gathering input for the president's evaluation from the representatives of these groups has significant value. The input can be collected with a simple evaluation form, but it can be much more powerful in a formal face-to-face interview process. As a college board, consider inviting representatives from the various internal constituency groups for a short discussion about the performance of the president. The effective facilitation will involve having some topics queued up to direct the conversation. Advance sharing with the discussion group before the interview will help frame and focus the conversion. For instance:

- How is the college doing compared to last year?
- What is going well?
- What needs attention?
- How often does the president meet with you? Are these effective meetings?
- In what areas does your group need support?
- How are effective communications achieved with the president to keep your constituency group informed?
- How would you assess the president on the critical competencies and skills?
- What might the college president do more of, less of, or differently to help your constituency group achieve its goals

Defining a formal process can be useful to keep the conversation on topic. Without structure and a clearly defined process for constituency group input, the conversation could turn into a gripe session. That may occur, regardless. If so, listen and affirm that you have heard, but do not engage. Steer the conversation back to the formal process.

> A side benefit of constituency interviews is that it gives the participants an audience with the board. Typically, this only happens during a board meeting when constituency groups provide their formal reports to the board. The constituency interviews provide the attendees the opportunity to reflect on the college and the president and provide feedback directly to the board. There may be times where this input is critical in evaluating the performance of the president. It also sends a strong message that the college board provides meaningful institutional oversight per the board's charter.

The Formal Evaluation

The college board should prepare a formal document as a result of the evaluation of the president. A draft of the evaluation should be reviewed with the president before formal approval and finalizing the evaluation. This practice will allow discussion of any critical issues, concerns, and opportunities. In some cases, inaccuracies, insufficient information, or other items will need to be addressed further. The college board should then formally approve the evaluation and present it to the president. In some cases, the college board may also be required to send the evaluation results to state or local authorities as part of the annual college board oversight process.

> The strength of the evaluation is its effectiveness and impact over time. In any given year, there may be ups, downs, successes, and challenges. However, if done regularly and consistently, a pattern of institutional and executive improvements will be evident. The regular, consistent evaluation process is key to tracking and measuring performance accurately.

Selection, Hiring, and Removal of a President

Some community college boards have full authority and control over the selection, hiring, and removal of a president. Some have limited

14. A Solemn Duty

roles. Some have no role. Usually, hiring and firing of the chief executive is the most important role of a college board, and it is the college board's decision that has the greatest impact on the success of the college. That decision requires consistency and clear delineation of responsibility and process. With the recognition that these efforts are public and inherently political, and the selection of the president fundamentally affects all stakeholders, including faculty and staff, the community, and ultimately, the students.

With regard to these duties, the board's first responsibility is to have a clear and undisputed understanding of its role, responsibilities, and limits. Imperative to the process is defining and documenting a comprehensive, clear, fair, and legal process. The process should be vetted by human resources, legal counsel and other regulators.

When Is It Time for a President to Leave?

Several factors can result in the need to make a change in the office of president:

- The president is retiring, has resigned, or has accepted another job;
- The president is in poor health or cannot otherwise carry out the job responsibilities;
- The president is no longer effective in the job, improvement seems unlikely, and the condition appears to be terminal;
- The president has done something inappropriate enough to necessitate removal.

As is apparent, several of these are likely beyond the control of the community college board and therefore attention shifts to the next president. The college board may play an active and meaningful role in the transition of presidents.

 The bottom line is this: if the college board determines that the president can no longer effectively lead the college and improve the college's performance, then it is likely time for a change.

Can a Negative Situation Be Fixed?

The college board should assess whether or not the current condition is terminal. A well-done presidential evaluation process can go a long way to help clarify the effectiveness of the president over time: Is this finding an anomaly? Unexpected? Is the current situation consistent with a trend of increasingly poor performance? Can it be fixed? If not, the college board should move decisively and quickly.

Alternatively, for a serious situation that might be remedied, honest and respectfully frank discussions should take place regarding the current situation—cause and effect, actions moving forward, and expectations. This means clarifying in detail for the president:

- the current unacceptable or unsustainable situation;
- the root causes and responsibilities of the concerns;
- corrective actions with specific measures and deadlines; and
- the consequences of failure to act as prescribed.

Termination of the College President

Regardless of the precipitating events, discussions regarding termination should be a formal and respectful process. The college board should consult with the college's (or community college system's) human resources department, employment and labor attorneys, the system office, or other experts to ensure that proper procedures are understood and followed.

Specific college board action upon the removal of the president depends on its role and scope of authority. The board may vote to terminate employment or formally request a formal resignation, or the board may approve a resolution of non-confidence that is then forwarded to the party responsible for any final action. Be aware that much of the process will be public record or at least in the public view. So proper public relations should be considered and managed.

In any case, the termination of a president's service is a difficult, but critical, responsibility of the college board. The board's highest priority is to hire and support an effective college president.

Presidential Transition

All planes land eventually. Likewise, all community college presidents will move on. Unless it is absolutely necessary to be immediate, a proper and thoughtful transition can tremendously benefit the college and the incoming president. The college board may want to meet with the outgoing president to reach an understanding of transition expectations, some of which might include:

- updating the status of significant projects or initiatives (stop, start, hold, postpone);
- avoiding direct report staff changes;
- defining direct report staff transition responsibilities;
- avoiding unusual or significant expenditures;
- supporting and orienting the president's successor;
- agreeing to a schedule of time off (unused leave);
- defining any future role that the outgoing president may have with the college.

Search, Interviews, Selection, Introduction

At some community colleges, the board is fully responsible for finding, selecting, conducting negotiations, and hiring the new president. In others, the college board supports the process on behalf of local governments or a system office. Regardless, the first step is understanding the college board's role and responsibility in the process. The college board policy and procedures manual should contain a clear description of this function.

Search and Selection

The college board is likely not alone in this process. State or local human resources departments often have established procedures that may provide support for the presidential search and selection. The board may opt to appoint a search committee to support most of this process. Regardless of the process, most presidential searches share key features:

Preparation

- Review and update the position description
- Outline the "perfect candidate" relative to the college's culture, current and future needs, and foreseen challenges

- Review the position's compensation and perquisites
- Develop criteria for applicant written or oral presentations
- Possibly engage a search firm to help advertise, screen, background check, and vet preliminary applicants

Screening

- Eliminate all but the most desirable two or three candidates by the search committee though applicant portfolio review
- Conduct onsite visits to the college for full interviews and presentations to the college board and key constituency groups
- Hold stakeholder events and local visits for the candidates and their families

Selection

- Rank and select the finalists
- Negotiate (compensation, perquisites, starting date, etc.)
- Publicly announce the next president of your college

Orientation of the New President

So, you have hired a new president. Congratulations!

Supporting the presidential transition contributes to a successful debut and may well lay the groundwork for a successful presidency. The college board may consider these ideas:

- Brief the president of any critical, current, or emerging issues that might require early attention
- Meet with the president as a board to discuss the state of the college (strengths, weaknesses, opportunities, threats)
- Arrange formal meetings with key community leaders such as local chambers of commerce, economic/workforce development organizations, leaders in the business community, and K–12 and university leadership in the college service area
- Host stakeholder events and other informal gatherings to introduce the incoming president to the full board, the foundation board, education leaders, local officials, state elected officials, and others

14. A Solemn Duty

- Coordinate with the president and family to support their house hunting, school selection, and neighborhood selection

 When the college board takes the lead in these orientation and transition activities, it not only helps the new president to hit the ground running; it also serves as a critical endorsement from the board of the new college executive.

Key Chapter Takeaways

- Document the college board's role and responsibility for the presidential evaluation process early in the president's tenure.
- Document the college board's role and responsibly for the presidential *firing* process before it needs to be used.
- Document the college board's role and responsibility for the presidential *selection and hiring* process before it needs to be used.
- Document the college board's role and responsibly for the new college president's *orientation* process before it needs to be used.
- Remember: the president's evaluation is not just for the bad times. It should be done regularly and periodically from the time the president starts. That practice alone may go a long way toward avoiding future problems.

Chapter 15

Last Impressions

Leaving the Presidency

When a President Leaves

On the first day as president of a community college, you probably do not put much thought into your last.

However, there will be a last day.

It is prudent for all good executives to plan for that day to the benefit of the community college, the students, and constituents.

Knowing When It's Time to Go

Many college presidents have said privately something like "I no longer find myself getting up in the morning with fire in my belly to go to work!" or "I just don't have the passion for being president and I'm weary of the demands of the job."

Regardless of the specific phrasing, the message and conclusion are the same. It is time to think about making a major life change—retiring, or phasing into another type of work.

Many presidents who reach this conclusion have been outstanding leaders. Those who are the most fortunate reach this acknowledgment before it is too late, while they can still leave at the top of their game. One of the worst experiences that a college president can have is to stay too long as they feel their enthusiasm wane and fade away, and both the president and the institution suffer.

> You may have heard that instead of someone working for five to ten years, they worked for one year, five to ten times.
>
> This scenario is not pleasant for the president, and often results in a loss of momentum for the college. In the worst case, the engagement of the college leader declines to a level where the

president is no longer among the key thought leader in the community, resulting in the college no longer being at the table for major community initiatives.

Spreading the Word
(Date, Process, Communications)

Few processes prove more impactful for a college than transition of the college presidency. Once a president has decided to make the major life change of leaving the presidency, it is important that there be a well thought out plan to initiate the process and inform all the stakeholders about the decision. Numerous "right" ways to go about communicating this decision exist; however, there are clearly "wrong" ways to go about it as well.

Whether the college organizational structure is that of the president reporting to a chancellor or directly to the college board, it is critical that the president meet with the chancellor and the college board chair to inform them of the decision, to discuss timing, and a develop a game plan for communicating and implementing the transition. Typically, if the president is leaving on his own accord, the time from the date of public announcement to the president actually leaving and the successor president starting is about six to nine months.

Because the president cares deeply about the college, he/she will want to contemplate seriously what is in the best interest of the college in the timing of their transition. This is not an exact science. In most cases in the community college world, six months is adequate for the chancellor or college board to go through the process of finding a successor president. In other cases, and for a variety of reasons (e.g., the college is located in a less desirable location to live and where it is difficult to attract a robust pool of presidential applicants, etc.), it might be necessary to allow nine months or more for the process of finding the presidential successor.

Whatever plan is developed for announcing the transition, it should be coordinated with all internal and external communications to faculty and staff, to college and foundation board members, to key stakeholders, and to the community at large. The form and timing of making such an important announcement is critical so that both internal and external stakeholders feel they are valued and are among the first to know about this upcoming change.

Challenges of the Lame Duck Period

Being a lame duck can be a somewhat uncomfortable experience for the president who has been in charge for years and who is accustomed to having faculty and staff being attentive to anything the president has to say. Upon delivery of the transition announcement, the relationship between the college president and the faculty and staff will be forever changed.

It would not be accurate to imply that the exiting president is demoted in the minds of faculty and staff, but it is human nature to develop some level of anxiety over the change. Concerns about the uncertainty of their personal future (as well as that of the college overall) since they do not yet know who the next president will be, what the priorities of the next president will be, and/or whether their jobs and security will be impacted by the transition are natural reactions. Remember that change of any sort is stressful for many people. The exiting president will feel a shift in the relationship with faculty and staff at their college. They can no longer plan ambitious long-term initiatives since their tenure is short-lived.

Within weeks of the announcement of a transition in college presidents, and as part of the transition plan, exiting presidents will need to consider their relationships with external stakeholders, organizations and boards. In some cases, the exiting president might be serving on a community board with an upcoming reappointment scheduled that would not likely make sense for the president who is leaving. Some organizations are structured in such a way that it is the college president *by title* who serves on their board. In other cases, it is the individual *by name*. In either case, the president will need to transition off boards in a way that is in the best interest of the organization being served, as well as of the college.

The Presidential Search Process

In most cases, the college board owns the presidential search process. Even in cases where the college board contracts with a presidential search firm to manage the search process, the college board controls, approves, and is in charge of the presidential search.

 It is important for exiting presidents to understand that the entire presidential search process is about the future of the colleges after they are gone.

15. Last Impressions

The search process itself is managed by the college board and there is very little need for the exiting president to engage, meddle, attempt to influence, or in any other fashion, engage in the process of selecting the successor president, unless specifically asked by the college board.

This can be a bit complicated and awkward at times, especially if an internal candidate wishes to apply for the presidency. Complications can arise whether the exiting president is supportive or unsupportive of the internal aspiring president.

Be aware, throughout the search process, in which there is much interest by staff at all levels, people will approach the exiting president for information about the search, how it is going, who the candidates are, how a particular candidate might be doing, and so on and so on and so on.

This potential complication reinforces the need for the president to stay out of the process and leave the mechanics strictly to the deciding entity—and to make that position entirely clear to all concerned.

A Smooth Transition: Interaction with Successor President

This element of a presidential transition can be a tricky one. In fact, having asked two chancellors what their advice would be to a president who is leaving the presidency, both stated two things:

1. "Don't make any key hiring decisions of executive staff nor any major decisions for the college; leave it for the incoming president."

2. "Give the successor president your phone number, email, and any other contact information. Invite the incoming president to contact you should they need to."

"Do's and Don't's of Exiting the Presidency

1. DO coordinate the announcement of your leaving with the chancellor and/or college board chair.

2. DO develop a communications plan with a timeline to announce your departure to the faculty/staff and the public.

3. DO give the incoming president your contact information and invite him/her to contact you should they wish to discuss anything.

4. DO NOT make any critical hiring decisions once the decision has been made to leave the presidency.

5. DO NOT make any significant financial decisions or commitments and leave them for the incoming president.

In all likelihood, you will never receive a call from your successor. Without reading anything negative into this, simply accept it as acknowledgment that you have done a superb job and the next president assume leadership and move the college to the next higher level of success... without you (as it should be!).

Key Chapter Takeaways

- Recognize that presidents tend to stay too long in their presidency rather than leave too early.
- Accept that once the announcement is made that the president is leaving, the relationship will be forever changed with faculty and staff.
- The exiting president should not have *any* engagement with the search process for their successor—leave that to the college board.

Chapter 16

Sea Tides or Tsunamis?
Emerging Threats

Challenges are coming. Being true to your principles, seeking solid counsel, and following process are critical to overcoming these challenges. This chapter covers some recognized emerging threats to help prepare and react.

Some days it feels as if you are drowning. You might be saying to yourself, "if they would only just let us teach!"

The seemingly constant barrage of newly discovered responsibilities, unfunded mandates, and emerging threats can be overwhelming. The pace at which these new issues reach your desk seems to increase as each day passes.

Still, as cliché as it is, these threats are opportunities, and they represent inevitable change. If your community college does not react to the ever-changing community needs, it will become irrelevant to the community it serves.

You have lifelines. The president, college board, executive cabinet, and other stakeholders can work together to keep everyone's heads above water.

The key is having constant awareness of your college's community roles and responsibilities, then determine how best to meet them in the changing landscape. A periodic SWOT (strengths, weaknesses, opportunities and threats) analysis might be enough to keep you afloat and help ensure you focus on what matters. Some threats represent something new. Others are always lurking…

Personnel Issues

People…. What are you gonna do?

You are in the people business. You need people as customers (students). You need people to teach. You need people to help manage the people. People are complicated.

Personnel issues are very complicated. Between ADA, OSHA, EEOC, FMLA, ICE, numerous regulations, and privacy issues, anyone can easily misstep. You need HR professionals. A strong director of human resources is critical to your community college. This professional will help you and your college stay on top of regulations and best practices. This multi-focused manager can:

- ensure that fair policies and procedures are in place ahead of difficult situations;
- screen, hire, and fire to help your college build and maintain the best staff;
- help cultivate and improve the workplace culture;
- lead and support your professional development efforts to strengthen the local workforce;
- mediate conflicts in a fair and equitable way;
- help ensure that lawsuits are avoided; and
- have a significant influence on the culture of your college.

Inevitably, despite this support, you or a staff member may make a serious mistake. The key is to not panic, brief your human resources director, and trust the professionals before you act.

 Most would agree that the day you fire someone is a bad day for you and them. This is true without regard to the reason

Policies and procedures should be well established so that whoever is being fired is not surprised by the action.

Still, most will not take the news well and many react poorly.

Work to maintain the dignity of the employee being fired.

Let them leave without being humiliated in front of their students, their peers, and their community. Sometimes that just means privacy. Sometimes, it is simply paving the way for a resignation or retirement. Understand that being fired is humiliating. Work to change the public perception, regardless of the termination cause.

Private, For-Profit, and Non-Profit Propriety Schools

Frankly, this competitive canvas can be perplexing.

In many cases, the local private, for- or non-profit two-year proprietary schools routinely attract a number of your prospective students.

This is despite significantly higher tuition for an equivalent curriculum. Why are students and their parents willing to pay more?

Much of this has to do with marketing and packaging. These schools;

- often have large media and advertising budgets;
- typically have newer, more opulent facilities;
- typically offer more flexible schedules and semester systems;
- often target their advertising to a uniform consumer;
- often advertise (what appears to be) job placement guarantees; and
- are very effective in using state and federal student aid programs to eliminate the tuition discrepancies.

Enrollment Pressures

Shrinking enrollment can be financially paralyzing to a community college. The obvious reason is that state and local funds are often directly tied to enrollment numbers.

However, that is not all. Capital expenditures, including new facilities, are tied to capacity. If your student population is not growing, it is hard to justify adding capacity.

There is more. If your enrollments are dropping, it sends a signal to the community about your contribution to the community. If fewer students are showing up, do we really need you? Maybe the marketplace is screaming that someone or something else can better meet the workforce needs.

Enrollment shrinkage is an existential threat.

It is easy to blame outside, uncontrollable causes, such as:

- The high-school graduation demographics are working against us.
- Our marketplace just saw two for-profit colleges open.
- The economy is good; people do not need to retrain for a job.
- The localities just opened a regional CTE campus.

You cannot succumb to this thinking.

Countless companies and organizations buck trends and increase market share when their peers are losing customers. Therefore, it is imperative that you strategically address the admissions issues and develop tactics to overcome them. Consider...

- Can you improve your marketing campaign?
- Can you form stronger relationships with your referral pipeline (high schools or local business)?
- Can you target underrepresented demographics or geography?
- Can you identify and eliminate obstacles to a sale (admission bureaucracy)?
- Can you follow-up with dropouts or no-shows?
- Can you modify your course offerings to better meet the current community needs?

Data-Driven Decision-Making—If You Don't Know, Don't Do It!

Data rules. It can also kill.

You will often find yourself in a meeting about a current challenge. Someone asks about some underlying facts:

- How many students does this affect?
- Is this number stable or changing?
- How does it measure across demographics?
- What are the contributing factors?
- What do the students say about this?

Before you know it, the issue is tabled until data can be vetted, analyzed, and the questions answered. Studies commence, surveys are sent out, and number crunching is in full bloom. By observing this process, you seek a better understanding of the underlying issues, and hope to make an informed, data-driven decision.

Good plan.

The problem is that at the subsequent meeting, more questions will likely emerge. "I see that it affects more women, but our women population is growing. So, is this growth proportional?" and "Shouldn't we also ask students that only take the classes at night?"

The cycle continues. Your inaction is due to analysis paralysis.

We are not suggesting that you do not need the data. The issue is that there will *always* be more questions. The hope is that with these data you can predict the future. Well, you cannot. You should be informed, but there are practical limits. The Pareto principle suggests that you probably know what you need to know sooner than you think. Gather the key data points, make inferences where needed, and be informed by the data you have. Act. Then, as always, be prepared to pivot if reality belies the data you have.

Helicopter Parents ... Always Watching, Just Out of Reach

Students will have challenges and problems. A student may:

- be missing class;
- be missing assignments;
- have performed poorly on an exam;
- not get along with their project groups; or
- not get along with an instructor.

Many students will talk to their parents about their problems. Many have learned that their parents can often solve their problems for them. Some parents have learned that if they speak up loudly, they can get positive results regardless of the underlying issues. Often, the suggestion is that the college, the instructor, or fellow students are treating their child unfairly. The student's failures are not their fault, but rather someone else's. Many parents provide cover for their children, hovering over them like a helicopter, ready to swoop in and attack.

Instead of consulting the student on an issue and encouraging them to take responsibility, you find yourself addressing the "outraged" parents. They make it clear that this is not about their student getting up early for a class or not turning in an assignment, but rather your failure to make special accommodations to their child.

Often parents will escalate issues to the dean, the college president, or a board member. The parent may call in a favor to a well-placed political figure.

This kind of parental involvement is not new, but. if not managed appropriately, it can be paralyzing to the college.

With few exceptions, the key here is to react quickly to ensure that the parent's concerns are heard, but leave it to your faculty and staff to resolve the issue and respond to the parent. That may just mean referring a phone call to the instructor, asking them to respond immediately and keep you informed. If you call the parent back, or worse, fix the problem, you will encourage this behavior, undermining your fellow professionals. A follow-up with the instructor (or their manager) might be warranted to ensure your staff and faulty understand the need to take all issues seriously. You also do not want to be caught off guard if you get a call from the governor should the parent escalate the issue to their important friends.

Some parents will land the helicopter, understanding that sounding the alarm on behalf of the student is ultimately not helpful to their child. Other parents have been intervening for their kids since kindergarten. They will most likely not change.

With all student issues, remember to comply with FERPA (The Family Educational Rights and Privacy Act of 1974) to ensure the confidentiality and protection of your students.

The key is to help *all* students succeed in a fair and equitable manner, recognizing that some need more help than others and some need more help at different times in their lives than others. Do your best to recognize that the helicopter whirl is noise.

Getting Ahead of a Crisis

When faced with a crisis, it is common to hunker down.
You can find yourself paralyzed because of the unknowns:

- How bad is it?
- Who will be affected?
- Will we survive this?
- How long will it last?
- What's our next step?
- Do we have existing policies that address this and if so, what are they?
- ...and then what?

With these questions looming, it is easy to wait and say, "no comment."
Likely, that mistake will only undermine your college's ability to work through the crisis.

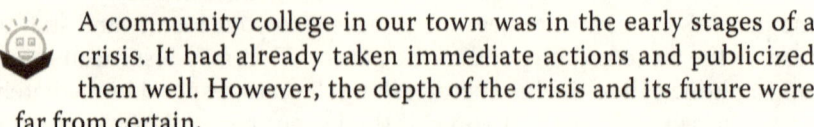
A community college in our town was in the early stages of a crisis. It had already taken immediate actions and publicized them well. However, the depth of the crisis and its future were far from certain.

The college was concerned that the lack of a clear and complete message was leaving students worried about their future with the college. They searched for something that would alleviate their student's angst.

The college *took the bull by the horns.*

They formed a "telephone tree" and called *every* student.

They told them what they had already done, what they thought next steps were, and what risks lay ahead. They were frank regarding their uncertainty of the future.

The students reacted well to the phone calls, the transparency, and the honesty. They were willing to be patient and to wait for next steps, confident that the college had their best interests in mind.

Bureaucracy Creep:
The Kudzu of Higher Education

Bureaucracy, not a friend to community colleges, comes in many forms, shapes, and sizes. It can significantly affect the collective and individual workload and place a strain on the human resources of every college.

The federal government recognized this issue with implementation of the Paperwork Reduction Act of 1980, designed to reduce the paperwork burden the federal government imposed on private businesses and citizens. Ironically, the act itself contained nearly 10,000. That being said, in today's litigious society, there would be no question about the importance of having written policies that protect both the individual and the institution from lawsuits and provides guidance.

"Bureaucracy creep" is a reality for every community college. Although it cannot be fully contained, college leadership must make every effort to minimize the amount of time and energy it takes to comply with the multiple entities that require paperwork, information, and reporting (hardcopy, online, or both). Of course, the reporting needs to be accurate and well presented, as it reflects on the image and reputation of the college. More importantly, this paperwork documents actions and helps the college avoid negative repercussions of being out of compliance.

For example, a community college in a large statewide community college system had a four-inch-thick college policy manual. In addition, the community college system office (the chancellor's office) also had a four-inch-thick statewide policy manual. As you might expect, much of the information was redundant. Although the information is now available online, to the user the volume and duplication still feel cumbersome, and create challenges that can be time consuming.

All community colleges, whether small, medium, or large, urban, suburban, or rural, have relationships with federal, state, and local governments that are sources of funding and other resources. Where there is a statewide community college system, the state legislature awards an appropriation to the system that becomes part of the system's budget. The state system then assigns monies to individual colleges based on a defined funding formula.

In cases of community colleges that are not part of a statewide system, the most common scenario is that the counties/city that make up the service area of the college provide funding through local taxes. These governmental jurisdictions, of course, have fiduciary responsibility and provide some oversight of funds awarded to the college, in addition to financial audits (and in the case of the federal government, financial aid audits). Although common sense dictates the need for systematic oversight, this imposes additional bureaucracy on the institution receiving the funds.

Accrediting bodies also add significant bureaucracy to the workload of community colleges. In the case of accrediting bodies for community colleges, the regional accrediting bodies accredit the entire institution and allow those institutions access to federal financial aid (under Title IV of the Higher Education Act of 1965) for their students. The regional accrediting bodies that serve community colleges include:

- Middle States Association of Colleges and Schools (Middle States Association or MSA)
- New England Association of Schools and Colleges (NEASC)
- North Central Association of Colleges and Schools (NCA)
- Northwest Commission on Colleges and Universities (NWCCU)
- Southern Association of Colleges and Schools Commission on Colleges (SACSCOC)
- Western Association of Schools and Colleges (WASC)

Other accrediting organizations exist to accredit specific academic programs. These entities are often found in health and technical fields. Their approval serves as quality endorsement that adds credibility to the students who complete the program. Others serve college operational areas and offer standards of compliance, such as a police department with the Commission on Accreditation for Law Enforcement Agencies, Inc. (CALEA) or Virginia Law Enforcement Professional Standards Commission (VLEPSC).

All of these organizations are essential to the college because they are sources of funds and/or a source of quality control, ensuring proper standards are met for the students. They are all helpful in developing and maintaining high quality in the work of the college, but they do consume faculty and staff time... a drain on human resources.

The message here is to reduce bureaucracy whenever possible.

How bureaucracy is managed becomes part of the culture of the college, and without proper management, bureaucracy will increase slowly over time and eat away at time that can be better used for other things. After all, most faculty and staff already feel that their workload is too great and that it seems to be increasing. In other words, manage the kudzu before it harms the landscape.

24/7 Cloak of the Presidency— The President Can Never Really Take It Off

Although it is very possible for the college president to go home at night to enjoy some personal time, it is important to remember that the "cloak of the presidency" is always visible to others.

Most people never get to know the college president personally, but he/she is well known generally in the community and the citizens naturally think of the institution when they see the college president. As a result, anything the college president does can reflect on the college.

One president shared a personal story that when he was taking a vacation in Germany and had gone into a local pub for some beer and brats, when he walked out, not plastered but certainly feeling a bit tipsy, a young man walked up to him and said, "How wonderful to see you here in Germany! I'm a student of yours back at your college!"

Another president shared his story of mild embarrassment when he was attending a large community event at the local downtown convention center on a very rainy evening. When he aggressively wrestled his car into the public parking garage, outmaneuvering another car to get in, he discovered that the car he had aggressively cut off belonged to the chair of his college board. Although they laughed about it later, it caused a brief moment of embarrassment for the college president.

Although there is no need for paranoia about the presidential cloak, it would be wise to remember that whether or not you can feel the cloak on your shoulders, it is always there and visible to the community. Wear it wisely!

Managing a Staff in the Digital Age: Remote Work

With increasing digitalization, much work and study can occur remotely. Classes can be taught entirely online. Cloud-based administrative systems can run from any computer, anywhere in the world. Staff and faculty can attend meetings virtually. What impact does this have on your community college?

Virtual participation, while efficient and expedient does not allow for the casual collaboration, taking in the body language, enjoying the ease of group participation, or sensing the room's mood. That being said, with some care, virtual participation can be almost as effective. It can certainly help overcome expenses or other challenges to business to continue with minimal interruption.

In some cases, supporting virtual presence may simply be an accommodation for when someone cannot be physically present. A student is not feeling well, but could attend remotely. You call an important "all hands on deck" staff meeting, but several staff members are on vacation or away at a conference. You hold convocation at one campus location with remote viewing at the others. Preparing for these options can facilitate participation that might otherwise be impossible. In some cases, allowing remote participation may be necessary to hold the event at all. Early on, these remote participants will likely not have the ideal virtual experience. You will need to work though glitches, camera angles, sound and light tweaks, screen sharing, and other issues. As you do it more, you will discover successful practices.

Like most challenges, the use of virtual technology also presents an opportunity. The Best practices come to the fore as you provide more virtual experiences. They will serve you well as more and more participants come to expect remote participation. Soon it will become the standard. When that happens, you:

- may be able to hold class or a counseling session during a blizzard or other campus-closing event;
- will find cost and time savings by eliminating travel;

16. Sea Tides or Tsunamis?

- will find it easy to routinely record sessions for those who have scheduling conflicts;
- will likely see more participation as the burden of travel is replaced by simply propping up in bed;
- may rethink your next building or expansion, recognizing the reduced need for collaborative spaces; and/or
- may be able to repurpose traditional classroom space for facilities that require a hands-on, present experience.

COVID-19 Pandemic

As this book was coming to completion, COVID-19 had paralyzed the country. As the threat loomed, with unknown effects and conflicting directions from leadership, it was hard to know what to do. Students, faculty, and staff were left unsure as they tried to fulfill their roles at the college and be safe. No one was prepared.

With so much coming at you early in a crisis, you do what you have to. For many, that meant closing the college completely with no real plan on reopening. Between students simply not showing up and faculty/staff who were at home with their out-of-school children or from concern for their safety, offering classes as usual was not an option.

The next step was communicating with your board, staff, faculty, students, system office, and other stakeholders to share what you do know, what you do not know, and what you are doing. That could include:

- No one is permitted on campus.
- No date set regarding reopening.
- No decision on how exams will be handled.
- No decision on how current semester grades will be affected.
- Next update announcement scheduled for one week from today.

These decisions do not need to be made in a vacuum. Listen to local, state, and federal government, health agencies, your peers, your board, your faculty and staff, your students. You may not get it right the first time. As you learn more, adjust.

After the initial shock and response, you start to see more clearly. Maybe the students can return if we have fewer, smaller class sessions, enforce the use of personal protection, and offer more online classes.

Before you know it, you are planning for the next session.

The point is not the decisions you make. Rather, it is what you can learn and improve upon in your crisis management. Once the dust settles, assemble the college board and your senior staff to perform a post-mortem on your reaction, planning, communication, and response. Determine what needs to be in place for an improved response for you or your successors during the next crisis.

The Unrelenting Need to Keep Up with Technological Advances

New tech is sexy.

You go to a conference. A salesperson makes a presentation. You read about it in a journal. Wherever you find it, the typical reaction is:

- I have to get one of those.
- That will solve so many problems.
- The staff would love it.
- The students will love it.
- We can use it in our marketing.
- The other presidents will be jealous.
- We will be trendsetting, cutting edge.

Much of that may very well be true. The problem is that there will always be something new. The promise rarely meets expectations. Soon, it too, will be obsolete. Chasing technology is expensive and time consuming.

That does not mean all technology is bad. It just means you need a decision-making process and criteria for purchase and adoption. Ask yourself:

- What portion of the student body will actually benefit from this?
- What portion of the faculty or staff will actually benefit from this?
- What is the total cost of ownership?
- What does complete success look like?
- What does complete failure look like?
- What are some alternatives to purchasing the tech that would achieve the same benefits?
- Will this increase our capacity? Our curriculum?

- Will this better serve our community?
- What is in the best interest of our students?

Like most decisions, it is not about a specific purchase or action. It is about adopting a formal, effective, systematic decision-making process. Again, you need professionals to make good decisions about technology options.

How to Think About and Prepare Your Institution (and Yourself) for the Future

John W. Martin
President/CEO, Southeastern Institute of Research, Inc.

U.S. birthrates indicate that your future students will be older. There will simply be fewer young people. Now is the time to begin preparation. That means catering to second careers, retirees, lifelong learning, and professional development.

Between changing birthrates and immigration trends, our country is headed toward a minority-majority. That means adjusting your college's cultural perspective. It likely means adapting to more students from homes where English is a second language.

More importantly, as the traditional source for new customers (young students just out of high school) shrinks, colleges will close. Preparing for a more competitive higher education marketplace, adjusting, and contributing will be the challenge. In short, change is coming, keep an eye on future trends and consider proactive changes.

> It is not the strongest species that survive, nor the most intelligent, but the ones most responsive to change.
> —Charles Darwin

Financial Pressures

Financial pressures are a constant. So much is beyond your control, like:

- State control over tuition rates
- Local control over tuition rates
- Local tax revenues and contributions
- Capital investments and longtime deferred maintenance needs
- Federal and state student financial assistance
- Competitive market pressures

Significant changes in any of these could mean layoffs, fewer class sessions, discontinuance of programs, and other difficult actions with long-lasting consequences.

The key to managing this is to find, attract, and retain an excellent financial director. This professional will:

- be frank with the president and the board as a trusted advisor;
- understand the opportunities and nuances of public funding options and maximize your college's share;
- learn to recognize future trends and prepare for them;
- maintain a conservative fiscal policy so that inevitable financial surprises do not force rash decisions;
- recognize the long-term effects of cuts or windfalls on current and future budgets;
- steer the college towards capital expenditures that have lasting benefits;
- ensure that the college is adhering to all applicable financial controls and management; and
- work with federal, state, and local agencies in transparent and cooperative audit processes.

Reality Versus the Perception of Reality

The college president and the college board members must not lose sight of the ever-changing dynamic of reality versus the perception of reality.

The community college president is often the person people both inside and outside of the college look to for decisions, direction, and clarification of a position or issue. This may involve, for instance, a personnel issue about to evolve into a grievance to a massive movement that has overcome the nation and now is impacting the college.

16. Sea Tides or Tsunamis?

Often people will look to the president for wisdom and fairness in settling issues, recognizing that most issues have multiple dimensions with a confusing mix of both reality and the perception of reality. Importantly, it is the perception of reality that often is more impactful to the many constituencies involved.

> Remember that most issues have multiple perspectives that often have conflicting or very different points of view. The reality of a situation may be very different from the perception of reality, and it is often the perception of reality that is the more powerful driving force in the moment.

What follows is a true story that illustrates the dynamic of reality versus the perspective of reality.

Part One: The Good Samaritan

My wife, Nam, and I went to play golf one Memorial Day late afternoon, and when we were on the first green getting ready to putt, a baby goose came running up to us, young enough that she didn't have colored feathers and had only a soft brown cottony fluff. Not knowing what to think, we finished the hole, got into our golf cart, and rode to the second tee… waddling behind us, as fast as her little legs would carry her, was this baby goose.

After ensuring that I would not hit the gosling, I played the ball down the fairway. Nam did the same. The gosling continued to follow us. At that point, I picked her up and held her close. She promptly pooped on my shirt (no good deed goes unpunished!) and I carried her to the pond next to the green and tossed her into the water, thinking she would find her comfort and paddle away. She swam for about ten seconds and then climbed back up on shore and followed us to the second green. Nam and I continued to putt out and finish the hole.

And yes, as we drove to the third tee-box, behind us was the rapidly waddling baby goose. I told Nam I knew that mother geese were quite protective of their infants. This must have been a case where the baby got lost or something serious happened. We decided to pick the baby goose up, leave the golf course with her, and go home.

Soon after, we took our pontoon boat out to find a gaggle of geese with the hope that this little one might be adopted. In short order, we came across about 30 geese floating in the lake in a large mass. We approached the gaggle, tossed the baby goose into the water, and then turned our boat around as quickly as we could and left. The baby goose seemed to be comfortable swimming among the other geese, so we left feeling good and hoping that the other geese would adopt our new found baby. It was one of those good feelings... the good feeling of saving an innocent and adorable life.

Part Two: Discovery and the Right Thing to Do

Nam and I went home. I changed my shirt, and we returned to the golf course and started over again, hoping to get nine holes in before sunset.

Upon reaching the first green we saw a woman walking around the side calling out "Annie! Annie! Come here, Annie!" and she turned to us and called out "Have you all seen a baby goose anywhere?" Uh oh!

Nam and I agreed that we could not tell her what had happened as we didn't know if we could find the baby goose again. The woman said that Annie had lost her mother and that she was raising her until Annie grew wings and could be given her freedom. I turned to the woman and shouted back "We will help you find her!" So, we turned the golf cart around and went back home for the second time.

Not knowing what to expect, we got into our pontoon boat and headed back to where we had let Annie loose to join the other geese. The geese were not where we left them. We drove our pontoon boat down the lake looking for a gaggle of geese. After crossing the lake and looking along the shoreline, we spotted the geese in a large lawn on a hill across the lake. As we approached, we could see Annie comfortably sitting in the middle of the gaggle with the more mature geese on the hillside eating grass.

Part 3: Annie Goes Home

We pulled our pontoon boat up to the edge of the shore and called out, "Annie, Annie.... Come here Annie!" And guess what? She raised her head, looked our way, and began walking through the other larger geese and down the hill, jumped into the water, and swam up to our boat. I picked her up and held her, and told her we were taking her home again.

We drove our pontoon boat back home, jumped back into our golf cart, and headed back to the golf course (for the third time). We found the woman walking a fairway and told her that we had found Annie and had brought her back home. The woman and her son were so very happy that they we on the verge of crying.

A happy ending to an unusual story. However, the reality of what had happened was never known.

16. Sea Tides or Tsunamis?

Political Pressures

Political pressures and learning to manage them are part of life for anyone in a leadership position. At a minimum, political pressures are sea tides in continuous ebb and flow, with the size of the waves varying significantly and the political winds sometimes shifting with little warning. Although it is rare that the political waves reach tsunami stature, from time to time they do, and it can be devastating for the college president and even for the institution as a whole. The college president must maintain a neutral position in politics and live and work in a manner that is respectful of all major political ideologies as much as possible.

Politics is fundamentally a form of relationship-building, a primary role of both the college president and the college board. At the federal level, members of the U.S. Congress provide millions of dollars of financial aid and scholarships (student loans, Pell Grants, etc.). Congress determines how much federal funding is available to public institutions versus private proprietary schools, a fierce private sector competitor for public monies.

States provide appropriations to community colleges in many states. This funding must be approved by state legislature, and the control of the state legislature can swing back and forth at any time between the Democratic or Republican control. We can all think of times in the past when the control of state politics has swung back and forth between the two major political parties. And although it seems commonsensical, it is important that any advocacy for dollars focus on the impact that community colleges have on changing people's lives for a better future: a universal value of community betterment.

In addition, and although not spoken about bluntly except behind closed doors, community colleges are in great competition with the four-year public universities in the world of funding. There are only so many dollars to go around. The four-year universities have several advantages in lobbying for state legislative support.

Most state legislators have never attended a community college and in many cases, their children have not attended a community college either (although many of their children will attend one for a short time, but consider it history after transferring to a four-year university). Four-year colleges and universities have athletic teams and the on-campus living experience which resonates in the hearts of students and adds pages to their memory books of great times in their lives. Four-year institutions have robust alumni associations that continue to nurture the relationship for years after a student has left the university, a common practice being to provide lifetime use of a personal email account with the name or letters of the university being part of the email address (e.g., nameorinitials@depaul.edu, nameorinitials@stanford.edu, or nameorinitials@harvard.edu) thereby creating an almost subliminally enduring reminder of the connection.

Dr. Monty Sullivan, President of the Louisiana Community and Technical College System, stated during an interview that "People love universities because of how they feel when they are part of their university. People love their two-year college for what we do, and not for how we make them feel." The community college relationship with legislators (and donors) is more transactional and less about how you feel. This directly relates to political pressures, because the relationship with state elected officials can impact the funding for community, so the college president must identify and reinforce over and over and over again the "value-added" (transactional gain for voters) by providing monies to their community colleges.

At the local level, especially for community colleges that have a locally-appointed college board and receive funding from local tax monies/assessments, the politics of relationships with local elected officials must be managed well. The relationships need to be strong, and although it is easier for local officials to understand and appreciate the positive impact of their local community college on the residents and the community as a whole, there are so many competing needs for funds that it is essential to find ways to reinforce those relationships continuously.

Future Challenges from the Board Leadership Perspective

James Cuthbertson
Former Board Chair, State Board for Community Colleges of the Virginia Community College System

First, I must state that this is neither a scientific treatise on higher education nor a scholarly examination of the many facets of our overall system of education in the United States. It is an attempt, however, to suggest that there are monumental issues facing higher education today that can best be addressed and changed for the better only by leaders within academia and their boards. Moving forward with discussions about the mechanisms available, the reorganizations necessary, and a path to greater success in our educational systems are critical to the very survival of dimensions of our higher education system.

As I considered my charge to reflect upon the impact and importance of both advisory board and state board interactions with newly appointed college presidents, I was drawn to the many factors that distinguish exceptional leadership in community college presidents and, for that matter, society in general. To accurately assess opportunities for the success of new community college chief executive officers, it is important to first discuss the characteristics of their successful boards and how they may achieve success despite the challenges facing our traditional approach to educating America's leaders.

It is imperative that community colleges, universities, and college systems populate their governing boards with the most visionary and mission-driven leaders available. Exceptional leaders recognize the value and gifts that others bring to the table. They are not threatened by other competent and successful team members. They readily share information and use their influence to advance the careers of their colleagues for the good and betterment of the organization.

Exceptional leaders are life-long learners and remain accessible and approachable. They are of a high moral character and are accountable throughout their tenure for their actions and decisions. Likewise, they are held to high standards in all their professional endeavors.

They are skillful and competent in the art of organizational design and governance. They have an outward perspective by understanding the role and position they play in the larger cosmos of their discipline and their stature within the decision-making hierarchy of their institutions and higher education systems.

By having an "outward perspective," exceptional board members are readily recognized as visionaries. They acknowledge that the future belongs to those individuals and organizations that embrace change. Those who see, espouse and chart courses that will move their organization to positions of prominence despite the chaos and risks associated with innovation and departure from the safe confines of the status quo. They are the ones who will prevail. Those leaders are the ones who accept the challenges to their organization's safety and success willingly and eagerly. They recognize that the high price of success is often less costly than the price of remaining stagnant in an ever-changing landscape.

Exceptional board leaders recognize those forces that are moving to impact the success and, oftentimes, the very existence of their organizations. They understand the threats and opportunities that present themselves in the kaleidoscope of forces impacting the community college systems throughout this country and higher education in general.

They will act. Ignoring the forces of change impacting the community college system is a non-starter. The higher education system of the United States will most likely undergo a realignment in the not-too-distant future. How academia delivers its "product" and in what domains will be the subject of much discussion in the coming months and years.

The advent of the internet has led to the explosion of remote learning. Distance learning offers a multitude of opportunities for those who are unable to travel or too remote from the campus. They have been a boon to sagging college tuition revenues, and offer expanded systems and approaches to learning in new fields of studies.

Higher education is becoming digitized. Courses leading to terminal degrees are available on laptops. Exams and student evaluation are completed in the absence of the instructor. Online education has been recognized as a valuable and meaningful learning experience through which students can gain experience, where video conferencing and instruction becomes the dominant mode of instruction.

Henceforth, how many of the buildings and teaching facilities that now adorn our college campuses will be required to fulfill the mission of the system to educate future students? What of the array of student services offered on campus? Will the need for some of these services lessen or be completely negated by this realignment of the teaching nexus from the campus to the home?

There are other more direct, threatening forces and conditions that leaders in higher education must address as they position their organizations for success. The outright survival of the community college concept, constructed 60 years ago for a non-homogenous population, is worthy of contemplation.

U.S. college and university enrollments continue to decline. Not all institutions have been affected equally: four-year public and elite private institutions continue to grow, while small colleges and community colleges, in particular, missed their goals for enrollment and tuition revenue over the past few years. It is projected that community college enrollments will continue to decline, particularly in rural areas of the state where college-age populations have been declining for the past decade.

The erosion of enrollee numbers may be permanent reality. It will manifest itself in the excess capacity costs of half-empty community colleges in the long-term. This decline in student enrollment alone will bring into question the viability of a system of community colleges uniformly distributed around the state without regard to the demographic potential that each area holds for sustained student enrollments.

On another front, pressure will continue to be brought upon colleges and universities to rein in tuition increases and to justify unspent endowment funds that could be used to ameliorate the rate of tuition increases.

Larger universities and private colleges will continue to receive great pressure to spend endowments, grants, stipends and other fellowships in support of tuition reductions. As you know, community colleges have no opportunity to benefit from stables of collegiate wealth; nor do they have the opportunity to participate in federally-funded research and other grant programs at the same level as their four-year college and university brethren.

Despite the efforts of colleges and universities to demonstrate value, not only in employment and earnings benefits but also in their role as a regional economic engine, the access and cost factors continue to enter the discussion of the need for a college education. Many of these arguments support the skilled and certificated workforce as the bedrock of the community college mission.

Related to the discussion of value, there is growing concern about employment and job placement. Students and parents increasingly expect their college or university to be a partner in helping them to map out a successful career path. Recent studies have found a gap between student expectations and college performance in career placement.

In that light, are there opportunities to expand internship/apprenticeship-type relationships with major employers for those soon to graduate or wrapping up their final course work? Will major regional employers be willing consider adding workplace scholars to complete the core requirements of specialty degrees or certificate programs?

Our education system needs help in its challenge to prepare the next generation of globally competitive American workers. Improving our educational system will require new ideas, more effective use of resources and innovative strategies to supply industry and commerce with a trained workforce. Help already comes from a variety of sources. Leading corporations have decades of experience in addressing their needs and the voids not being filled by a dependable stream of candidates for critical positions.

These corporations recognize that to remain competitive in today's global economy, schools must produce graduates who are not only competent in math, science and reading, but who also possess critical thinking skills, communication abilities, and a global mindset.

The issues fulfilling these critical workforces will force the private sector to devise its own training programs and seek partnerships with willing academic centers. As they expand their view of how future candidates will fill critical needs, academic centers can respond by "work hardening" and programs designed to fill industry's needs.

With their performance records and expertise, businesses have great resources and motivation for success. Every day, business leaders manage complex departments and systems while leveraging finite resources, all the while lobbying policymakers and bureaucrats to create business-friendly environments that attract new businesses and support enterprise expansion.

Just as they tackle underperforming business units, corporations can bring their considerable skills to bear on improving the United States' system of education. Is there a "best" way to channel this critical corporate effort? Probably not. There are many faces to our complex system of higher education. Regionally tailored programs and industry specific initiatives will most likely find the greatest favor.

So, where does the visionary academic leader go from here? They must acknowledge the changing landscape of higher education and recognize those negative forces impacting its success. All of that must be on their institution's docket. The visionary leaders will be academia's change agents. They will challenge conventions and find substantive ways to improve retention and graduation rates, lower student costs, and increase the return on their college's investment.

Visionary board leaders will support the pursuit of innovative and collaborative partnerships with major employers. These opportunities will illuminate new opportunities while they advance mutually shared goals of higher graduation rates and a more skillfully trained workforce. They must get out ahead of the issues. The community colleges that best weather challenging storms are those that anticipate and confront issues early and honestly.

I have discussed only a few of the challenges facing our education system in this country today. What will become of our systems of higher education in the coming years is up for grabs. We all know that it must change.

 ## *Key Chapter Takeaways*

- There will be future unexpected threats or even crisis. What is important is that you have an institutional process to recognize them and then deal with them.
- Some threats are existential. Have your antenna tuned for these.
- When a new threat emerges, it can feel like crowds are gathering at the gate demanding a solution. In reality, the issue is probably more important to you than it is to the imaginary crowd. Your constituents will appreciate a well thought out assessment and resolution over a quick action.
- Before it becomes necessary, develop a public relations/press/social media strategy. Ensure that everyone understands *who* speaks for the college and *when* a designated individual speaks. The person may vary, for example, from an admissions perspective to campus police.
- HR and finance departments are complicated. Find the skilled and trustworthy professionals to ensure your college is properly managing these essential areas.

Chapter 17

SYSK

Stuff You Should Know About Applying for a Presidency

Author's note: If you are a fan of the podcast *Stuff You Should Know* (SYSK), you will appreciate this chapter. Applying for a college presidency is a unique experience. Through experience and research, we have distilled down the critical needs for a successful presidential search and interview process in this chapter.

After reading the previous chapters, if you still find the idea of becoming a community college president exciting, then you should find what follows to be of great benefit. Moving forward and taking this chapter to heart would suggest that you have done your personal due diligence, weighing the pros and cons of the demands of the position, of the personal time that a college presidency will take away from your family, of the never-ending political pressures that come with the job, and of that feeling of backing a noble cause but forever swimming upstream, being asked to do more with less.

If after all of that you still have the fire in your belly, then take heed of the content in the rest of this chapter. It will help you get your first presidency.

Fire in the Belly and the Disney Song "It's a Small World"

The competition is tough for a community college presidency, and you will be competing head on with others, some of whom have placed this goal as a top priority. Some applicants will be intensely passionate and so excited about becoming a president that, similar to competing in sports, their adrenaline increases, their focus intensifies, and they commit their body and soul to the goal. Be warned now that on a scale of one to 10 (10 being high), if you find your passion to be anything less than a nine, don't bother applying or going through the process. You most likely would not survive it!

Believe it or not, although there are approximately 1,200 community colleges throughout the United States and the number seems impressive it really isn't so big. Search agencies and consultants eventually learn the names of sitting presidents and applicants, and when they see an applicant applying for many college presidencies at the same time, large and small, urban and rural, geographically spread out, they can begin to wonder whether the applicant who has taken a shotgun approach, feels desperate and is not seriously considering the continuity between his/her personality and the individual colleges.

Once you have reached the point where you definitely want to begin applying for a presidency, contemplate those things that are most important to you. Write them down, and explore presidential postings *without compromising your top priorities.*

 Going through a personal assessment of your top priorities for a good match between yourself and a community college presidency can be similar to house hunting.

When my wife and I are in the house hunting mode we create a list of those things that:

1. We cannot do without
2. We would like to have
3. We don't care about, one way or the other

For us:

1. We have a small dog, so having a fenced (or fenceable) back yard is a must and we would not consider a house without it.
2. We would prefer a double car garage versus two single car doors; but it is not a deal breaker.
3. Whether or not the kitchen has an island really doesn't matter to us.

Would you prefer a small single campus college where everyone gets to know everyone else and it has more of a family feel, or, would a large five-campus institution in a large urban area have more appeal? Are you fine living in a part of the country that has long and cold winters or do you need a more temperate climate?

These are things you cannot change, so your thinking needs to be clear from the beginning and you should *not* apply for any presidencies that do not meet your top-level priorities. Waiting it out and seeking a good match will result in greater happiness in the long run and more likely, success in your presidency.

Casting a Net ...
How Big Should the Net Be?

In the fishing world it is said that if you cast a broader net, you will catch more fish than with a smaller net. There is likely much truth to the thought, however, that *where* the net is cast is much more important than the net's size. Whether the net is large or small, if it is cast in an area where there are few fish, it will not catch fish and you will not reap the rewards. This is also true with the college presidential search process, and it is critical to remember the more important factor here is not the number of applications submitted, but the closeness of the match between your personal priorities, strengths, and skills with the college's leadership needs.

Avoid the temptation to apply for any and every college that is in search of a new president! You may end up with a presidency that is not a good match for you, sort of like marrying the wrong person when you know before getting married that you are wrong for each other and that it isn't a good match. Such a marriage usually ends up being a disaster and ending in divorce.

How Will You Know If You Are
Ready for a Presidency?

There is no way to measure objectively how ready a person is to be a college president. Individuals with experience in the more traditional career paths of academic affairs and/or student affairs have usually been exposed to a broad scope of college operations. The common scenario is for to begin one's career at a lower level position and work his/her way up the ranks. In these cases, the individual has usually performed the work of the institution at various levels and understands the dynamics of a specific operational area. By the time a person reaches the vice-presidential level and serves on the college president's executive cabinet with other senior administrators, he/she would most likely have interacted significantly with people who lead the operations of most of the other areas of the college.

Since you don't typically wake up one day and just decide that you want to be a community college president, when you first begin to have such thoughts, observe those around you in senior leadership positions and specifically observe your college president. Since every community college presidency is different, think about what you might do and how you might respond if in the president's position. Remember that being human, no college president is perfect and they all make mistakes. Also, every sitting college president was a brand new president sometime earlier in his/her career.

> If you find yourself having thoughts about a community college presidency yourself, take the time to sit with your current president and discuss what the president's life is like. What is it like on the good days? What is it like on the days that are less than good? What time and energy demands does the president feel? How much of the work of the presidency is political?
>
> You might even askwto set up a shadowing experience for one day a month in which you spend the day with the president to get a sense of how he/she interact s with other leaders in the community and what a day in the presidency is like. No two days are alike for the college president.

Faculty-Speak: Crossing Over to the Dark Side

GLENN DUBOIS
Chancellor, Virginia Community College System

The term often used tongue-in-cheek by teaching faculty, "crossing over to the dark side" is a reference to a college faculty member who teaches and then leaves that role to become an administrator. Even so, as Glenn DuBois, chancellor of the Virginia Community College System (who has hired many community college presidents over the years, and fired some too), pointed out in a February 2002 lecture, some of the very best administrators come from the college teaching ranks.

Administrators who were former college teachers tend to never lose sight of the complexities and dynamics of the classroom. They know what is needed from the administration to help teaching faculty be more successful with their students. They fully understand the cadence of activity and demands on teaching faculty throughout the academic year, which may not be fully understood by those who have never actually taught nor spent time in the classroom. And, they can both empathize and sympathize with the many stresses and demands experienced in the lives of most community college students. Chancellor DuBois' conclusion is that "in general, former community college teachers make the best community college presidents!"

Overcoming Not Having Fundraising Experience

Most first-time community college presidents do not have formal fundraising experience, and yet they seem to survive it as their presidential experience matures. Think about it this way—even those who are the very best at something had to do it for the first time at some point in their life!

As described in an earlier chapter, fundraising is a combination of both art and science. The science side of the equation is something that everyone can study. Fundraising is a somewhat linear process with the steps clearly defined almost in a formulaic fashion: identify a critical need, develop a case for support, identify potential donors, etc.

> If you are already in a senior position at your community college and are contemplating someday becoming a college president yourself, ask your current president and vice president/director of institutional advancement if they will ask the foundation board to appoint you officially to the college foundation board. You will be expected to give some money to the foundation, but it would most likely be a reasonable amount and well worth the investment.

Doing so would put you "at the table" and engaging with the fundraising experts of your college and your community. You would learn the process and dynamics of raising resources (money and other resources) in a more formal way. It would also give you an opportunity to observe even further the college president and how they interact with both the foundation board and the vice president of institutional advancement. It would give you experience interacting with donors as well.

And lastly, if you take this step a year or so before you begin applying for your first college presidency, when you are asked in an interview to talk about your fundraising experience you will be able to look the search committee members in the eye with confidence, describing your experience on the foundation board and the successes that you were part of during that time. You will also be articulate in discussing fundraising concepts like "the ask," and "donor pyramid" and other lingo common in the fundraising world.

Sources for Presidential Job Postings

There are multiples sources for identifying which community colleges are currently in a presidential search process. One source is the website of a community college in presidential search mode, where there is usually information about the search (including the application process and timeline) on the front page of the college's website. A couple of other good sources are *The Chronicle of Higher Education* and the *Community College Daily* (an online list provided by the American Association of Community Colleges). And lastly, if you have developed a social network with other community college professionals, such information is often communicated personally by word of mouth or on social media.

Pre-Presidential Opportunities to Sharpen Your Readiness to Apply

For individuals who are good planners and think ahead about preparing themselves for a community college presidency, there are two excellent "boot camp" programs for aspiring presidents.

Executive Leadership Institute (ELI) of the League for Innovation in Community Colleges

The Executive Leadership Institute (www.league.org/eli2020) provides the opportunity for prospective community college presidents, or those in transition, to analyze their abilities, reflect on their interests, refine their skills, and engage in leadership discussions with a successful community college leader from across North America.

Future Presidents Institute (FPI) of the American Association for Community Colleges

The Future Presidents Institute (www.aacc.nche.edu) of the American Association for Community Colleges provides hands-on experience for senior leaders aspiring to the community college presidency. The association has gathered years of research from CEOs about what they wish they had known before assuming the presidency. The faculty for the institute is drawn from the community college leadership field and are highly skilled presidents, chancellors, and groundbreaking leaders. Institute faculty leverages their community college leadership expertise and field-based practical skills to create new knowledge and enduring concepts that shape the practice of community college leadership.

The FPI competency focus areas are specific categories identified as having significance to the internal and external workings of the community college. The 11 focus areas are:

- Organizational Culture
- Governance, Institutional Policy, and Legislation
- Student Success
- Institutional Leadership
- Institutional Infrastructure
- Information and Analytics
- Advocacy and Mobilizing/Motivating Others
- Fundraising and Relationship Cultivation
- Communications
- Collaboration
- Personal Traits and Abilities

Raison d'être *of Your Resume*

Your resume has two (and only two) purposes. One is to be a master depository or archive of every professional position you have held throughout your working lifetime, hopefully documenting in great detail both your responsibilities and accomplishments as you moved throughout your work experiences. The second purpose is very simple... to get you an interview!

It has become somewhat predictable now with the doctoral students I teach in community college leadership, that when we get to the part of the class where we discuss the presidential search process, at least one of two (or both) deficiencies surface related to their resume. Most students have not kept their resumes (or curriculum vitae) up-to-date, or if they are up-to-date, they are somewhat general and do not record enough detail to be helpful as they prepare to apply for their next position. For those who have not been diligent archivists of their previous work experiences, it can be very difficult to go back in time and recreate much of the success of the past without missing a lot. If your resume has been kept as a "master resume" then you can always go back to that source, save it under a new file name, and delete that parts that you do not need for a specific use or application. If you have not kept a detailed master resume, at a minimum, take two-three weeks to create a master resume that you can shape into a dynamic document that will help you in the presidential search process.

The second observation about resumes is that almost everyone builds into their resume what their job responsibilities were, but they do not include their accomplishments in the position.

> A two-word job title says it all when chatting with a stranger on an airplane... but not in a competitive job search process!
>
> We occasionally find ourselves sitting next to a stranger on an airplane and frequently the question is asked "What type of work do you do?" When the response is "I'm president of [insert name] College," there would typically be little doubt in the other passenger's mind about what the college president actually does. It would be assumed and understood that the president did things presidential. Maybe the conversation would evolve into discussing sports or some other aspect of the particular college or university, but rarely much detail about the president's specific responsibilities. People generally know what the responsibilities of a college president (or vice president of academic or student affairs) are, but what they don't know is what successes a particular college president has had.
>
> Accomplishments need to be listed and highlighted in detail in an effective resume to be highly competitive in the presidential search process.

Due Diligence Before Your First Interview

Once you are asked to travel to the college for an interview (sometimes the interview is via video call or other technology), learn as much about the college to which you are applying as possible. It is very different if you are applying for the presidency where you already work, or at another college in the same community college system or state, but too much due diligence is much better than not enough. It is especially critical if you are applying for a community college that is out-of-state or one that you have never been to before.

> Go the extra mile with your personal due diligence about the college to which you are applying!

I once was contacted and asked to apply to a college in a different state. When the number of original applicants for the college presidency went from 65 to about a dozen, my cover letter and resume got me an interview. So as is typical, I received a call from Human Resources at the college to negotiate dates and travel arrangements for my interview.

At my own expense I went a day early. I spent the day in incognito mode, in casual khakis and a short-sleeved golf shirt, with my camera. I took the time to personally visit the college where I was applying to be president. In fact, the college had three campuses. I went to each campus during the daytime and walked around, observing everything that I could to get a feel for what it might be like to be a student or college president there. I went back to each campus after dark and did the same thing to get a sense of how I felt on the campus at night; whether I felt safe; if the lighting was adequate; if students seemed to be happy and engaged. I learned a lot!

But it didn't stop there. I traveled to two campuses of the nearest other community college and walked around their campuses as well (imagining both the competition and the opportunities for partnerships). Then I traveled to the large university that shared the same city as the community college and even traveled for over an hour to yet another community and visited the large land grant university just to get a feel for higher education in the state.

It paid off! The search committee knew that I was a candidate from out-of-state and they did not expect me to be very familiar with their college. But when they asked about my perceptions about their college, I was able to share with them the great effort I had gone to so I could be prepared and learn about both the college and the community. It can give you a positive edge if during an out-of-state interview you are able to tell them about the local barbeque hangout, or comment that students shared with you what they liked so much about the college. I guess it worked.... I spent 16 years as the president of that college, and left with president emeritus status.

Taking Things for Granted Can Be Deadly!

This happens most frequently when an internal candidate applies for the college presidency (or any other position for that matter). It is wise to treat the entire presidential search process as if you were an outsider. This includes not contacting people on the search committee and asking them for behind-the-scenes info on what the search committee is discussing, like which applicants are being favored, how you are faring against another candidate, or anything else. Remain "hands-off" in any inquiry with any personal relationship from the beginning of the search process until it is completely finished and the college board has either contacted you ready for an offer or they have publicly announced that they are hiring someone else.

If a formal presentation is required of finalists, prepare as if your life depended upon it, including providing the same level of detail that you would if you were applying for a college presidency far away from home. It is too common that an applicant treats the search process and search committee members as if they already know the strengths of the internal candidate. Remember, the search committee members know even better the weaknesses of an internal candidate, something that is still an unknown about other applicants from out-of-state. Never take things for granted!

Academic Qualifications for a Community College Presidency

Although there are some exceptions for community college presidents, it is typical that the community college president has completed a Ph.D., an Ed.D., a law degree, or some other "terminal" degree. At the four-year university level, it is not uncommon to find a former four-star general, a successful and retired politician, or a successful industry leader at the helm, but not so in community colleges. At a minimum, if you feel compelled to apply for a community college presidency, wait until you have successfully completed a good part of your doctoral program and calculate for yourself the burden of being a brand new college president, trying to finish the doctorate, and having some semblance of family life at the same time. In most cases with community colleges, the completed doctorate is a key that opens the door to be considered a qualified candidate for president.

While They Interview You, You Should Interview Them

The experience of traveling for a job interview is intense, and even after the travel and interview are over it is common that the whole experience feels like a blur. You will most likely remember key elements of the experience but not all of the details. The search committee has vetted you and you will soon find out if you made it to the next phase of the presidential search or if it has ended for you. The college will notify you.

Remember that while the search committee was assessing your candidacy, you were also (aware or not) assessing the fit for you if you were to go there as president. It is important for you to reflect seriously on how you felt (and still feel) about your experience. They may want you but it is equally and maybe more important that you are still excited about the college, the community, and the people you met during your interview.

I once applied for a first community college presidency at a small college in a rural part of the Midwest. My plans included traveling a day early so that I could scout out the community and be better prepared for my interview and I did so. Had I been offered the presidency; I would have turned it down.

First of all, I arrived the day before the interview after dark during a very heavy rainstorm. I located my hotel and made plans for the next day. When I traveled to the small center-of-town business strip that are common in small American towns in the Midwest, I saw that a third of the businesses were boarded up and had gone out of business. Upon driving to the campus and looking around, I observed that the concrete steps in front of the main academic building were all chipped, cracked, and in desperate need of repair. To say that the college campus was run-down would be kind. However, the thought occurred to me that it might also provide an opportunity. After all, it is sometimes easier to follow a president who has not done a good job than to follow the most successful president in the world. There are, of course, tradeoffs.

To make matters worse, on the day of my actual interview I was assigned a tour guide who happened to be the academic vice president who had applied for the presidency and didn't even get an interview. I guess it is sufficient to say that it wasn't the most inspiring campus tour that I had ever had!

And lastly, I learned later that when during the interview I made reference to a delightfully cheerful businessman who owned and ran the local barbecue hangout across the street from the college campus, that he was in a lawsuit with the college over something. Need I say more? Much of this I could not have learned without the personal experience of my visit. Due diligence for you as the candidate is very important!

First Impressions During an Interview

The concept of making a good first impression is basic common sense, but it is amazing how many candidates fail to make a good first impression when they show up for an interview. Below are a few obvious (but not so obvious for some) suggestions:

- *Eye Contact and Handshake*—If the world returns to handshakes after the COVID-19 pandemic impact, it is important to remember to look each search committee in the eye, shake their hand with a firm but not crushing handshake, and call them by name.
- *Appropriate Dress*—It doesn't matter how formal the culture of the college is, for the college president the expectation is professional business attire—a suit and tie for men.
- *Pre-study the Search Committee*—Generally the search committee members' names and titles are available as public information. It can be helpful to study the composition of the search committee members and imagine the areas of passion that individual committee members have.
- *Demonstrate Effective Listening Skills*—In some instances it can be helpful to repeat a question. This demonstrates the sign of a good listener and provides you with an extra moment to formulate your answer.
- *Sense of Humor*—Find a way (without being silly) to let the search committee know that you have a sense of humor. Effective leaders

have the skill of helping others feel at ease, and appropriate humor would be a very positive trait to have as the college leader.
- *Passion for Serving Students*—Above all, demonstrate a strong passion for students and be proactive in bringing the interests of students into your responses to questions. The core mission of any community college is to serve students, and faculty, staff, and board members all want to see their next president as someone focused on student success. Afterall, student success is everyone's success!

Follow Up After an Interview

It is not required but is a bit of a classy touch to send a "thank you" letter to the search committee within a day or two of the interview. It doesn't need to be lengthy, but rather genuine with a point or two about the most exciting observations about the college where your interview took place.

Personalizing a "thank you" letter can send a positive gesture back to the college.

I once learned during the final interview when the college search committee was down to three finalists that the local culture included wearing Hawaiian print shirts on Fridays, a tradition named after one of the beloved IT technicians at the college. Many people participated in this fun tradition and pictures were posted on the college website of faculty and staff wearing their Hawaiian print shirts every week.

Picking up on this fun local tradition while there with my wife for the final interview, the day after my interview and my wife having been given a tour of the city, we went to Walmart and purchased two Hawaiian print shirts, took a photo of us wearing those shirts, and sent it with a nice "thank you" note to all faculty and staff. It ended up being posted on the college website. People learned that I, too, like to have fun. It must have worked.... I got the job!

Compendium of Presidential Search Committee Questions

Chances are pretty good that the finalists for a college presidency are all qualified. So, a search committee interview may be the key part of the application process in selecting a new president.

17. SYSK

Search committee questions can cover a lot of subjects. Some are intended to get to know you. Some are intended to understand how you might handle current challenges should they give you the job. In any case, they are offered to allow you to distinguish yourself from the others applicants. **Preparation is a must if you are going to distinguish yourself.**

What follows is a sample of a few typical questions you might be faced with, along with some responses to consider. Review the list provided in the appendix and prepare your own answers as part of your interview preparation.

1. Why do you want to be president of [insert name] Community College?

I believe my background has prepared me well for a college presidency. I was looking for a good fit. The opportunities and challenges at [insert name] Community College are well suited to my strengths and interests. I especially like [insert specific observation] about the college. Based on that, I believe I can make a positive impact here.

2. What have you learned at your current college that would make you a better president?

In my current position, my responsibilities include a, b, and c. In addition, I have made extra efforts by a, b, and c to help better prepare me for the role of president. I am confident that my experience will benefit [insert name] Community College.

3. How would you increase and continue enrollment?

Despite pressures from a shrinking demographic and competition, there is clear opportunity for enrollment growth here. I believe opportunities in some of the underserved communities, older students, and workforce preparedness in alignment with some local industry needs present some great opportunities.

4. Describe your management style.

I would summarize my management style with several of my values:

- *I observe—management by walking around gives me the first-hand account of what might need attention and reinforces that I care about colleagues.*
- *I walk the walk—honesty, respect, transparency, and inclusion are behaviors I expect from both myself and the entire faculty/staff.*
- *I am accountable—I will prepare measurable goals and accomplishments for myself and the college and expect to be measured against them. These will be shared with all faculty and staff.*

A more comprehensive list of potential search committee interview questions can be found in Appendix A. Consider reviewing all of them prior to your interview and jotting down your thoughts. It will go a long way in your preparation.

Strategic Vision of an Applicant for President

Sharon A. McDade
Practice Leader for Strategic Services & Senior Executive Leadership, Greenwood/Asher, & Associates

When candidates interview for a presidency, one of the typical questions asked by the search committee is "What is your strategic vision for our institution?" This puts candidates in a bind. If a candidate expresses a clear and cogent strategic vision, committee members may discount the candidate for not having sufficient investment in involving members of the institution community in contributing to a strategic vision. If a candidate talks about the process and the belief that the institution's community should be involved in developing a strategic vision, committee members may discount the candidate as being wishy-washy and lacking in original vision. What is a candidate to do? Most candidates express default to expressing a general vision that showcases their ability to have a vision that is rooted in the mission and general sense of the institution, but with a caveat that, of course, they will refine that strategic vision once they get in the role and have opportunity to meet with faculty and other institution leaders.

Once in the job, the new president then faces a new strategic vision challenge—evolving in the articulation of a strategic vision while staying true to the general vision expressed during the search process—which was probably instrumental in the selection of the candidate as president. This leads to one of the most significant challenges of a new president: creating and articulating a strategic vision that can achieve buy-in from the institution's community while ensuring that the vision is packaged into an implementable and documentable plan. The answer has to do with strategic planning.

Some presidents inherit a strategic plan that they have to play out over a couple of years before they can put a new plan in place. Other new presidents enter an institution that has no plan or is finishing the final years of a plan and have to put in place a new planning process. Search committees and boards of trustees expect that strategic planning acumen must be an aspect of expertise that the new president brings to the institution. Some presidents have planning experience of some type, but many do not. Even if a new president has strategic planning expertise, what role should a new president play in planning? How much time should a new president devote to the leadership of strategic planning, given all of the other crucial or urgent tasks on the agenda?

Those presidents who inherit a plan face good and bad news. The good news is that they can continue to pursue a plan already in place, which, presumably, has institution community buy-in, while putting initial focus and energy into more pressing challenges and opportunities. The new president can use the time to get to know the institution, sort through the viability of senior members of the cabinet, and gain an understanding of the decision-making and buy-in processes of the institution. The bad news is that the new president has to live with a plan not of their own making for several years.

Those presidents who do not inherit a plan also face good and bad news, both involving needing to launch a strategic planning process sooner rather than later. Optimistically, it may always be good news to launch a fresh strategic planning process that will articulate a strategic vision of the president's own making. However, the new president may not yet have crucial cabinet members in place to be able to implement a new plan, and the institution may not have a clear concept of what a strategic planning process could or should be.

Often presidents engage their institutions (or, more specifically, their boards of trustees or senior cabinet) in developing a set of strategic directives. Such directives, typically expressed in a one-page infographic, provide a way to point an institution's community toward broad, agreed upon objectives. Broad objectives can be helpful in many ways, but because they lack the teeth of specific goals, metrics, and responsibility assignments they may not be sufficient to drive an institution forward.

The science, art, and expectations of strategic planning have evolved a great deal over the past decade. Increasingly, boards expect responsibility assignments for the accomplishment of goals and metrics against which progress can be measured, typically through a dashboard of trackable performance measures. There is little sense in having such a dashboard of performance measures if these are not backed by the specifics of a strategic plan that maps out specifically how goals will be accomplished.

What role should a new president play in strategic planning? There are many arguments and circumstances in which a president should directly lead the process. However, with all of the responsibilities and challenges facing a new president, there may be wisdom in assigning leadership of the planning process to the chief academic officer. This makes sense in that the bulk of the plan, ultimately, will have to do with the academic life of the institution. The provost can direct the planning process while staying in close contact with the president such that the president's strategic vision will permeate the plan. Whether led by the president or the chief academic officer, the plan will either be built entirely at the level of the board of trustees, the senior leadership team, or through a process that involves the entire institution community. Conducting the planning process at the level of the board of trustees or senior leaders can be quick, while involving the entire institution community will take longer. A strategic plan can be quickly built in a substantial retreat of the board of trustees or senior leaders. The community process will probably take an entire academic year.

A fundamental question for a president who is poised to undertake strategic planning is whether or not to use a facilitator. For most institutions, the last strategic planning process took place so long ago that memories of the process are faint. While there will always be members of the business college who feel that they have strategic planning expertise in the business world, there may be few people with expertise in strategic planning in higher education. A facilitator can bridge these experiential gaps and bring to the institution the current best practices in higher education planning. A facilitator may be able to save time and energy that might otherwise be lost in finding a way through the planning process by helping the streamline the process and by negotiating around barriers. A good facilitator will also help to develop the capacity of senior and unit leaders to work with a strategic plan and to engage with metrics to ensure greater success with implementation.

Ultimately, whether inheriting a plan or developing a plan, a new president will be measured against the implementation of the plan. A beautiful plan that sits on a shelf does not help an institution and may lead to short-term service for the new president. An implemented plan for which there is documentable progress against a plan's goals enables a president to ensure that a strategic vision guides an institution towards enduring success.

 ## *Key Chapter Takeaways*

- Apply for a college presidency only at institutions where you have great interest and the "fire in the belly" to fight for the opportunity. Avoid applying for any position for which your passion is only lukewarm.
- Take the time to write down the things that are important to you relative to where you would like to live and work and fundamental characteristics of where you enjoy working. Don't compromise or give up any of your top interests for a job. Be strategic in your search for a college that's a good fit for you.
- If you cannot get actual fundraising experience, then be creative in how you at least understand the science of fundraising and learn the lexicography and concepts so that you can speak intelligently about it. Search committees can understand that even the best fundraisers started out as beginners.
- Reshape your resume to highlight your accomplishments and not just your responsibilities.
- Practice responding to the questions provided in this chapter. You don't need to have a detailed answer for every question, but you do need to be prepared and not be caught off guard by questions.

CHAPTER 18

Help at Your Fingertips
Key Organizational Resources

This chapter contains a list of organizations that will serve as a resource for community college presidents, along with a short description of each organization, derived from the language on their websites.

Advocacy

American Association for Women in Community Colleges (AAWCC)
P.O. Box 3098, Gaithersburg, MD 20885
www.aawccnatl.org

The American Association for Women in Community Colleges (AAWCC) has long worked to ensure the equitable treatment and success of women in community colleges. Deeply rooted in the compelling access mission of community colleges, AAWCC champions the needs and interests of women students through scholarships, mentoring, and programming; advances the needs and interests of women working in community colleges through professional development, mentoring, and advocacy; and ensures the equitable and just treatment of women attending community colleges, working in community colleges, and visiting community colleges through advocacy, compliance, and awareness.

American Association of Community Colleges (AACC)
One Dupont Circle, NW, Suite 700, Washington, D.C. 20036
(202) 728–0200
www.aacc.nche.edu

The American Association of Community Colleges (AACC) is the primary advocacy organization for the nation's community colleges. The association represents nearly 1,200 two-year, associate degree-granting institutions and more than 12 million students.

Association of Community College Trustees (ACCT)
1101 17th St. NW #300, Washington, D.C. 20036
(866) 895-2228
www.acct.org

The Association of Community College Trustees (ACCT) is a non-profit educational organization of governing boards, representing more than 6,500 elected and appointed trustees who govern over 1,200 community, technical, and junior colleges in the United States and beyond. Located in Washington, D.C., ACCT is a major voice of community college trustees to the presidential administration, U.S. Congress, the Departments of Education and Labor, and more.

Community Colleges of Appalachia (CCA)
www.ccofapp.org

Community Colleges of Appalachia (CCA) is a voluntary association of public community colleges serving the common interests of member colleges and their communities through programs and services responsive to the unique cultural, geographic, and economic development challenges facing the region.

Best Practices, Innovation

COMBASE
COMBASE c/o CORD, 4901 Bosque Blvd., Suite 200, Waco, TX 76710
(254) 741-8331
www.combase.org

COMBASE, an abbreviation for COMMUNITY-BASED, is a consortium of many leading community and technical colleges in the nation dedicated to sharing innovative solutions to meet the challenges of our nation's rapidly changing economy. As a relatively small network of community and technical colleges led by presidents and chancellors, member CEOs and their staff members bring their best in innovative community partnerships, workforce solutions, adult education, and operational frameworks to the annual COMBASE fall conference.

League for Innovation in the Community College (LEAGUE)
2040 South Alma School Rd., Suite 1–500, Chandler, AZ 85286
(480) 705–8200
www.league.org

The League for Innovation in the Community College (LEAGUE) is an international nonprofit organization with a mission to cultivate innovation in the community college environment. League activities and initiatives center on essential topics for community colleges, including diversity, equity, and inclusion; information technology; leadership development; learning and student success; research and practice; and workforce development.

National Association of Community College Entrepreneurship (NACCE)
3434 Kildaire Farm Rd., Suite 215, Cary, NC 27518
(984) 238–2270
www.nacce.com

National Association of Community College Entrepreneurship (NACCE) is the nation's leading organization focused on promoting entrepreneurship through community colleges. The association represents more than 300 community and technical colleges and 2,000 faculty, staff, administrators and presidents who serve more than three million students.

Students

American Student Association of Community Colleges (ASACC)
2279 North University Pkwy, #165, Provo, UT 84604
(801) 785–9784
www.asacc.org

American Student Association of Community Colleges (ASACC) is a national organization that provides leadership, citizenship, and advocacy development opportunities for community college student government leaders. It is dedicated exclusively to the community college student leaders and strives to provide opportunities for students to network and share a common voice on national issues.

National Association of Student Personnel Administrators (NASPA)
111 K St. NE, 10th Floor, Washington, D.C. 20002
(202) 265-7500
www.naspa.org

The National Association of Student Personnel Administrators (NASPA) is the professional hub for the field of student affairs, dedicated to centering students in the evolution of higher education. The guiding principles of integrity, innovation, inclusion, and inquiry shape the work of fulfilling the promise of higher education for every student. By serving the field through exceptional professional development opportunities, research taking on the biggest challenges, advocacy for inclusive and equitable practices and communities, and nurturing networks and pipelines to mentor, rejuvenate, and support the career journeys of student affairs pros.

Curriculum

Community College Baccalaureate Association (CCBA)
575 Lake Bingham Rd., Lake Mary, FL 32746
(407) 463-2201
www.aacbd.org

The Community College Baccalaureate Association (CCBA) promotes better access to the baccalaureate degree on community college campuses and serves as a resource for information on various models for accomplishing this purpose. The association strives to gather all published articles and legislation dealing with the community college baccalaureate degree. CCBA also solicits copies of unpublished materials related to this topic and hosts an annual conference to share information and develop ways to promote the community college baccalaureate degree to governors, state legislatures, national policy boards, and other appropriate persons and organizations.

Community Colleges for International Development (CCID)
20515 State Hwy 249, Suite 11296, Houston, TX 77070
(281) 290-2909
www.ccidinc.org

Community Colleges for International Development (CCID) has

been helping members further their internationalization initiatives and develop globally competent workers since 1976. CCID engages and empowers an international association of community, technical, and vocational institutions to create globally engaged learning environments with the hope that all such institutions integrate international perspectives and experiences into their curricula and campus culture in order to develop globally competent students, faculty, and staff.

Community Colleges Humanities Association (CCHA)
c/o Community College of Baltimore County,
7201 Rossville Blvd., Baltimore, MD, 21237
(443) 840–5180
www.cchumanities.org

The Community College Humanities Association (CCHA), founded in 1979, is the only national organization for humanities faculty and administrators in two-year colleges. It is dedicated to strengthening and growing the humanities in two-year colleges as well as creating awareness of the value of humanities education for students, parents, employers, and members of the community. Since humanities study in higher education is not static, CCHA serves as a catalyst for defining and finding progressive solutions to the many fluid and mutable issues that face community college humanities faculty and administrators.

Instructional Technology Council (ITC)
19 Mantua Rd., Mount Royal, NJ 08061
(856) 423–0258
www.itcnetwork.org

The Instructional Technology Council (ITC) is an affiliated council of the AACC and represents nearly 200 institutions that offer distance education courses to their students in the U.S., Canada, and around the world. ITC is a leader in advancing distance education, and their mission is to provide exceptional leadership and professional development in higher education to its network of eLearning practitioners by advocating, collaborating, researching, and sharing exemplary, innovative practices and potential in educational technologies. ITC tracks federal legislation that will affect distance learning, conducts annual professional development meetings, supports research, and provides a forum for members to share expertise and materials.

National Alliance of Concurrent Enrollment Partnerships (NACEP)
P.O. Box 578, Chapel Hill, NC 27514
(919) 593-5205
www.nacep.org

The National Alliance of Concurrent Enrollment Partnerships is a professional organization for college and high school partnerships offering college courses in American high schools. NACEP works to ensure that college courses offered by high school teachers are as rigorous as courses offered on the sponsoring college campus. As the sole accrediting body for concurrent enrollment partnerships, NACEP helps these programs adhere to the highest standards so students experience a seamless transition to college and teachers benefit from meaningful, ongoing professional development. To advance the field and support our national network of members, they actively share the latest knowledge about best practices, research, and advocacy.

National Association of Community College Teacher Education Programs (NACCTEP)
2323 W 14th St., Tempe, AZ 85281
(480) 517-8000
www.nacctep.weebly.com

The National Association of Community College Teacher Education Programs (NACCTEP) serves as a voice for community colleges in national discussions about teacher education; supports institutions and individual members by enhancing current community college teacher education programs and serves as a resource for those looking to develop new programs; and facilitates connections between community college teacher education programs and faculty.

Development, Fundraising

Council for Advancement and Support of Education (CASE)
1307 New York Ave., NW, Suite 1000, Washington, D.C. 20005
(202) 328-2273
www.case.org

The Council for Advancement and Support of Education is the global non-profit association dedicated to educational advancement—

alumni relations, communications, development, marketing, and advancement services—and the goal of championing education to transform lives and society.

To fulfill their missions and to meet both individual and societal needs, colleges, universities and independent schools rely on and therefore must foster the good will, active involvement, informed advocacy and enduring support of alumni, donors, prospective students, parents, government officials, community leaders, corporate executives, foundation officers and other external constituencies. CASE helps its members build stronger relationships with all of these constituencies in a number of ways.

Council for Resource Development (CRD)
8720 Georgia Ave., Suite 700, Silver Spring, MD 20910
(202) 822–0750
www.crdnet.org

The Council for Resource Development (CRD) is the only professional organization concerned exclusively with fund raising for two-year colleges. Through education, advocacy and mentoring, CRD supports professionals and develops leaders engaged in community college resource development. CRD, an affiliate organization of the American Association of Community Colleges, serves more than 1,550 members.

Professional Development

Community College Business Officers (CCBO)
P.O. Box 80994, Charleston, SC 29416
(434) 293–2825
www.ccbo.org

The Community College Business Officers (CCBO) works to help business officers prepare for successful professional roles in the business and service enterprise of the community college. CCBO recognizes that excellence in the profession sets the standard for the future and strives to acknowledge those professionals who have excelled in the field.

National Council for Continuing Education and Training (NCCET)
9526 Argyle Forest Blvd., Suite B2–322, Jacksonville, FL 32222
(904) 466-9466
www.nccet.org

The National Council for Continuing Education and Training (NCCET) provides continuing professional education for staff of community, technical and junior colleges. NCCET is committed to providing its members with services that keep them up to date on new trends, help maintain a personal and professional network, and promote the latest leading-edge programs.

National Institute for Staff and Organizational Development (NISOD)
The University of Texas at Austin,
1912 Speedway, Stop D5600, Austin, TX 78712
(512) 471-7545
www.nisod.org

The National Institute for Staff and Organizational Development (NISOD) is a membership organization committed to promoting and celebrating excellence in teaching, learning, and leadership at community and technical colleges. NISOD provides faculty-focused programs and resources for community and technical colleges that want to make the most of their professional development dollars. NISOD is one of the country's leading providers of professional development for community college faculty, staff, and administrators.

Research

Center for the Study of Community Colleges
9544 Cresta Dr., Los Angeles, California 90035
(310) 951-3565
www.centerforcommunitycolleges.org

The Center for the Study of Community Colleges was established in 1974 in order to conduct original research pertaining to community college policy and practice. Previous Center projects have included the Transfer Assembly Project, the longest-standing study focusing on statewide measures of community college-university transfer, as well as national studies of community college faculty, student learning, assessment, and accountability. These and other projects were supported by grants from the Ford Foundation, the Carnegie Foundation for the Advancement of Teaching, the National Science Foundation, and the National Endowment for the Humanities, among others.

Community College Research Center at Columbia University (CCRC)
Teachers College, Columbia University
P.O. Box 174, 525 W 120th St., New York, NY 10027
(212) 678-3091
ccrc.tc.columbia.edu

The Community College Research Center at Columbia University (CCRC) studies community colleges because they provide critical access to postsecondary education and are uniquely positioned to promote equity and social mobility in the U.S. Its mission is to conduct research that helps these institutions strengthen opportunities and improve outcomes for their students, particularly those from underserved populations.

National Association of State Directors of Community Colleges (NASDCC)
1 Dupont Circle NW, Suite 410, Washington, D.C., 20036
(202) 728-0200
www.statedirectors.org

The National Council of State Directors of Community Colleges (NASDCC) is an affiliated council of the American Association of Community Colleges (AACC). The council provides a forum for the exchange of information about developments, trends, and issues in state systems of community colleges.

World Future Society (WFS)
www.worldfuture.org

The World Future Society (WFS), founded in 1966, is recognized as the largest, most influential, and longest-running community of future thinkers in the world. WFS members established the foundations of future thinking as we understand it today. Historical members and contributors included legendary minds such as Carl Sagan, Buckminster Fuller, Alvin Toffler, Herman Kahn, Peter Drucker, Arthur C. Clarke, Gene Roddenberry, and Margaret Mead.

Appendix

Compendium of Presidential Search Committee Questions

The questions listed below have been gathered from actual presidential searches. They demonstrate the breadth and depth of questions that are part of the interview process and provide insight into what you should be prepared to address when you go for an interview.

Prior to an interview, considering reviewing these and formulating responses as part of thorough interview preparation.

1. Why do you want to be president of [insert name] Community College?
2. What have you learned at your current college that would make you a better president?
3. What are your major strengths?
4. What are your major weaknesses?
5. How would you increase enrollment?
6. How would you begin your presidency at the college?
7. How would you work with local, state, and federal officials?
8. Describe your management style.
9. What is the role of the president?
10. Describe 3–5 major challenges facing community colleges in the next decade.
11. How would you maintain high quality educational programs with dwindling resources?
12. How would you serve business and industry in the college service area?
13. What experience have you had in developing high quality technical programs?
14. Discuss your experience with economic development.
15. What is the role of the board of trustees?
16. How would you envision president-college board relations?
17. What are the most important leadership qualities of a president?

Appendix. Presidential Search Committee Questions

18. Discuss your attitude and experience with affirmative action.
19. What strategies would you implement to encourage diversity among faculty and staff?
20. How would you motivate faculty and staff?
21. Describe your educational philosophy.
22. Describe your leadership philosophy.
23. Discuss your administrative experience.
24. How would you develop a positive relationship between the college and the community?
25. Discuss your course and curriculum development experience.
26. How would you develop institutional effectiveness?
27. What would you consider your greatest accomplishments?
28. What was your greatest challenge, and how did you handle it?
29. What new programs does the college need?
30. How would you market the college?
31. What are your personal long-term goals?
32. What CEO experience have you had?
33. How would you develop the college foundation?
34. What fundraising experience have you had? Describe successes and failures.
35. How would you handle changes and morale?
36. How would you balance technical and humanities programs?
37. How would you work with students?
38. Why should we hire you over someone else?
39. How would you improve the image of the college?
40. Demonstrate your abilities as a public speaker.
41. Describe how you see the community/technical college philosophy.
42. What is your background in the financial area?
43. Why should we hire you?
44. How would you deal with the equipment situation at the college?
45. Describe your decision-making process.
46. Describe the job of a two-year college president.
47. Describe your community leadership experience.
48. How would you develop successful off-campus centers?
49. How will you get to know people in the community?
50. Give examples of how you "get the job done!"
51. What management/leadership books have you read lately?
52. How do you problem solve?

Appendix. Presidential Search Committee Questions

53. How well do you see yourself getting along with the current vice president/academic dean at the college?

54. How well would you work with the local ethnic community of the college's service area?

55. What are some of the points in your educational background and professional experience that have best prepared you to be the president of [insert name] Community College?

56. It has been said that we learn more from our failures than from our successes. Share with us an example of a failure and what you learned from that experience.

57. Based on what you know about [insert name] Community College at this point in time, what would be your top priorities during your first three months as president?

58. As the new president, everyone will know your name. How will you get to know the students and faculty and other employees?

59. Please give us some examples of collaborative efforts you have established with businesses, community organizations, other educational institutions, and local government.

60. What are some ways that [insert name] Community College can work with businesses to enhance existing and develop new partnerships?

61. As our student body, college constituencies, and communities are culturally diverse, how would you manage to satisfy or balance the demands of all these various groups?

62. What have you done in your previous positions that has led to improved relationships among diverse groups (either internal college groups or community groups)?

63. How have you promoted a sense of community and trust in a culturally diverse institution? How might you begin that process at our college?

64. How would you handle a multicultural conflict resolution?

65. What strategies have you used to enhance professional development for faculty, staff, and administrators?

66. How would you encourage employees to become more committed to the institution?

67. What do you consider to be your biggest management mistake, and what lesson did you learn from that experience?

68. Please describe your interactions with students at your current institution. How would you interact with students at our college?

69. What would you see as your role as president in regard to our students?

Appendix. Presidential Search Committee Questions

70. Have you developed or implemented any programs that specifically address improving student success?

71. Please tell us about a new policy, program, or idea you recently implemented which was considerably different from the standard procedures. What approach did you take to get your employees to support it?

72. Can you give us an example of an important change at your college for which the initial impetus came primarily from the college board rather than from the administration or faculty? What was it and how did it play out?

73. Communications within the college and outside in the community are always an issue. Please give us some examples of communication strategies you have employed that have been successful.

74. What sources of information do you use to stay up-to-date within your current organization?

75. Please give us some examples of your experience in fiscal management. How have you dealt with budgetary constraints? How did you determine institutional priorities?

76. Please describe your experience working with collective bargaining organizations. If you have not had this experience, what do you expect might be some of the issues associated with such agreements and how would you deal with them?

77. Please give us some examples of working within an existing contract environment that was easy to adhere to, and when it was difficult to adhere to.

78. What types of strategies have you implemented to ensure a more inclusive decision-making process?

79. How have you recognized the productivity and contributions of various groups within your institution?

80. You have a new trustee on the college board. How would you define their responsibilities to them?

81. As college president, what would you do to make this campus a more exciting learning facility?

82. Please provide a detailed example of a problem you resolved using a participatory process.

83. Please describe the climate of "collective bargaining" or "shared governance" on your campus and your role in creating that climate.

84. Our [insert name] Community College is fortunate to have strong academic and technical divisions. What in your experience

Appendix. Presidential Search Committee Questions

has prepared you for the balancing, promotion, and governance of those similar yet dissimilar areas?

85. You have a new technical student before you who is signing up for the welding program. What would you tell this student when he/she does not want to take liberal arts courses like English and history?

86. What has been your experience in implementing technology in a two-year community or technical college? What technological insights do you have for our teaching, learning, managing, and communicating environment?

87. Please give an example of how current technology should be used in a progressive institution.

88. If cost was not a barrier, what technical improvements would you make to the college and the classrooms?

89. What measures should a community college take to ensure privacy and data security for both the students and faculty.

90. Please share with us examples of both positive and negative experiences you have had in working with faculty members to develop or implement new program ideas.

91. What, in your opinion, are the three most critical elements necessary to ensure student success? Why? How would you ensure that our students acquire these critical elements?

92. What evidence can you cite, from your professional record, of your commitment to affirmative action and equal opportunity? How would you carry out this commitment as president?

93. Please give us an example of a situation in which you served as a consensus builder, and an example of when you made a good unilateral decision.

94. How would you ensure that students and all employees have the opportunity to provide their input in decision-making?

95. Please describe your experience in the political process and what you consider to be the "A-B-Cs" of lobbying. What would you see as your role if you became president?

96. Please describe for us a great moment in your own education when you were a student. There are no limitations.... You define what is "a great moment."

97. How do you see the presidency of [insert name] Community College and life in the community fitting into your career, personal goals, and objectives?

98. As you know from reviewing the materials we have sent you and from the presidential profile, [insert name] Community College has

a strategic plan for the future. How do you feel about coming to a college with such an existing plan, rather than an institution which looks to its new president for vision and planning? How might you make an impact and put your own stamp on the strategic plan?

99. In your view, what is the most significant thing a college president can do to enhance the community's perception of the community college and the community college system?

100. The college board would like to become more involved in communicating with and recruiting in the minority community. How would you undertake such a task?

101. Describe an example of when you, as college president or vice president, disagreed with the faculty recommendation on a decision. Explain why you disagreed and how you handled the situation.

102. Community colleges are often described as "revolving doors," rather than open door institutions. What have you personally done to ensure strong retention programs for incoming students in your present (or previous) positions?

103. What was the most successful experience or incident you have had in working with teaching faculty, and what has been your biggest failure?

104. Can you provide a specific example of an issue which was supported by students and opposed by faculty and/or administrators? If so, how was it resolved? What was your role in the process?

105. What concerns have you encountered in working with a large number of hourly part-time employees? How did you resolve these concerns?

106. What is most attractive to you about the position of president of [insert name] Community College? What, if anything, is less attractive?

107. If you are selected as our president, how would you assess what is working well at [insert name] Community College and what needs to be changed? How would you seek information from a broad base of employees?

108. What is the distinction that you would make between the college president's (CEO) role and the chief financial officer's (CFO) role in planning and managing financial resources for the college?

109. As a leader, how would you create a "collegial" environment? Have you done this in your current position and how did you go about it?

110. What strategies, experience, or skills do you have that will help us develop a sound enrollment management plan?

Appendix. Presidential Search Committee Questions

111. Please describe the overall "customer service" attitude at your institution. How have you dealt with a specific department or person who was experiencing a problem in the areas of customer service?
112. What have you done to provide faculty and staff with professional and technical development in order to improve the quality of their teaching or work?
113. As college president, your time will have both an inward focus (having to do with operations in the college and student life) and an outward focus (having to do with fundraising, community engagement, and working with state and local government). How would you balance these activities?
114. Can you share with us an example of when you served as a facilitator or mediator between two internal constituent groups? How successful were you and, if you were not successful, what would you do differently?
115. How might you suggest that the college board be of best use to the institution in working with local governmental bodies?
116. What measures would you take to improve [insert name] Community College's ability to provide state-of-the-art facilities, faculty, and staff on the cutting edge of their respective fields?
117. Speaking from an administrative perspective, please describe the strengths and weaknesses of your current institution's governance system. What have you done (or would do) to address any weaknesses?
118. Describe an administrative initiative you developed that empowered others, encouraged innovation, improved morale, or promoted a climate of inclusiveness.
119. What has been your experience or involvement with business "incubators" or business resource centers?
120. How have you personally been involved in developing your institution's technology infrastructure and in bringing computing resources to faculty and students?
121. What methods have you used to ensure that administration, faculty, and staff are receptive and responsive to student needs? How might you begin the process at our college?
122. If you had to pick only three personal values as the most important for our college president, what three values would you pick?
123. What do you hope to be remembered for at your current institution? What do you think you probably will be remembered for?

Appendix. Presidential Search Committee Questions

124. Based upon what you know about [insert name] Community College, if you become our president, after three years, what would be different and what will remain the same because of your leadership?
125. What question do you wish we had asked you but didn't, and what about that would you like to share with us now?
126. Do you have any questions?

About the Authors and Contributors

The Authors

Mark C. **Creery, Sr.**, is the president/CEO of Data Directions, a technology company in Richmond, Virginia, that has been providing strategic IT application development and support since 1982. Mark has spent more than 40 years as a software designer, developer, and trainer.

He served on the college board of J. Sargeant Reynolds Community College for a total of 17 years, during which 5 of those years he served as college board chair. He was designated college board member emeritus upon his retirement from the board in 2020. In addition, Mark has served on several leadership boards in the Richmond area, including the ChamberRVA Executive Board, ChamberRVA Hanover Business Cabinet (chair) and Hanover County Economic Development Authority.

Gary L. **Rhodes** is a president emeritus of Reynolds Community College and an adjunct professor in Old Dominion University's Ph.D. program in community college leadership. Gary has a doctorate in higher and adult education and a master's in Spanish linguistics and literature, both from Arizona State University.

For more than four decades he invested his career in community college education, ranging from serving on a start-up team that built a brand-new community college in Maine to serving as college president in Minnesota and Virginia for a combined 20 years. During his career he also served on 33 community leadership boards in five different states and was chair or president of 12 of those boards, ranging from a large metro Chamber of Commerce, Rotary Club, several regional economic and workforce development boards, an arts council, an early childhood education board, K–12 strategic planning initiatives, business councils, and more.

About the Authors and Contributors

The Contributors

Sherrie Brach **Armstrong** is the president/CEO of The Community Foundation for a Greater Richmond.

Peter **Blake** is the Director of the State Council for Higher Education in Virginia (SCHEV).

John R. **Broderick** is the president of Old Dominion University in Norfolk, Virginia.

Benjamin **Campbell** is a pastoral associate at St. Paul's Episcopal Church in Richmond, Virginia.

Hara **Charlier** is the president of Central Lakes Community College in Brainerd, Minnesota.

Mary Elizabeth **Creamer** is the vice president of Workforce Development & Credential Attainment at the Community College Workforce Alliance in Richmond, Virginia.

James **Cuthbertson** is former college board chair/member of the J. Sargeant Reynolds Community College Board and former state board chair/member of the Virginia State Board for Community Colleges.

Glenn **DuBois** is the chancellor of the Virginia Community College System.

Siobhan **Dunnavant** is an obstetrician and gynecologist and currently serves as a State Senator in the Virginia State Senate.

Patrick **Farrell** is the former president/CEO of Doctor's Hospital in Henrico, Virginia.

Richard **Groover** is the assistant dean of the School of Mathematics and Science at J. Sargeant Reynolds Community College.

Dana B. **Hamel** is the founding chancellor of the Virginia Community College System.

Tim **Kaine** is currently U.S. Senator from Virginia and former governor of the Commonwealth of Virginia.

Jeffrey J. **Kraus** is Assistant Vice Chancellor for Strategic Communications for the Virginia Community College System.

James **Lane** is Superintendent of Public Instruction for the Commonwealth of Virginia.

David **Loope** is the president of Beaufort County Community College in Washington, North Carolina.

About the Authors and Contributors

Whit **Madère** is the former director of internal auditing for the State Community College Board of Virginia and is currently director of internal audit at the Archdiocese of St. Louis in St. Louis, Missouri.

John A. **Manzari** is a retired physician and former member of the J. Sargeant Reynolds Community College Board and former chair/member of board of trustees for Broome Community College in Binghamton, New York.

John W. **Martin** is a renowned futurist and the president/CEO of the Southeastern Institute of Research (SIR) and founder of the Boomer Project in Richmond, Virginia.\

Sharon A. **McDade** directed the Emerging Leaders Group and ACE Fellows Program at the American Council on Education (ACE) and previously directed Harvard University's Institute for Educational Management.

Stephen **Moret** is the president/CEO of the Virginia Economic Development Partnership (VEDP).

John J. **Rainone** is the president of Dabney S. Lancaster Community College in Cliffton Forge, Virginia.

Michael **Rao** is the president of Virginia Commonwealth University in Richmond, Virginia.

Theodore **Raspiller** is the president of Brightpoint Community College in Midlothian, Virginia.

Nam **Rhodes** is the spouse of co-author Gary L. Rhodes and supported community colleges and its president, interacting with college board members, college staff, working with the college foundation, and the community.

Stewart D. **Roberson** is the superintendent emeritus of Hanover County Public Schools in Virginia and the president/CEO of Moseley Architects in Richmond, Virginia

Kim **Scheeler** is the former president/CEO of Greater Richmond Chamber of Commerce in Richmond, Virginia.

Vaughn A. **Sherman** is a current consultant with the Association of Community College Trustees and the author of *Six Essentials of Good Board-CEO Relations* and *The Board Chair: A Guide for Leading Community College Boards.*

Edward **Steiner** is the former college board chair/member of J. Sargeant Reynolds Community College in Richmond, Virginia.

About the Authors and Contributors

Monty **Sullivan** is the president of the Louisiana Community and Technical College System.

Eugene **Trani** is the former president of Virginia Commonwealth University in Richmond, Virginia, and continues to serve as VCU President Emeritus and University Distinguished Professor.

Belle S. **Wheelan** is the president of Southern Association of Colleges and Schools Commission on Colleges (SACSCOC).

Index

academic qualifications 197–198
accreditation 23, 31–33, 66, 150, 172–173
American Association for Women in Community Colleges (AAWCC) 206
American Association of Community Colleges (AACC) 121, 194, 206
American Council on Education 14
American Student Association of Community Colleges (ASACC) 208
anecdote 7, 9, 11, 24, 25–26, 30, 38, 40–42, 45, 67–68, 133, 136, 139–140, 141, 170–171, 196, 198, 200
applying for a presidency 188–205
Armstrong, Sherrie Brach 102, 224
Association of Community College Trustees (ACCT) 61, 121, 207
audits 23, 71–72, 83, 172

balancing work and play 143–144, 147, 173–174
Blake, Peter 64, 224
board orientation 56–57, 78, 84, 87–88, 90
board policy manual 23–25, 78–79, 88–90, 171–172
brand new president 9, 47, 191, 198
Broderick, John 101, 224
bureaucracy creep 125, 168, 171–173
bylaws 11, 23, 78–84

Campbell, Benjamin 103, 224
Carver, John 54
Casagrande, Frank 13
Center for the Study of Community Colleges 213
Charlier, Hara 14, 224
collective bargaining 68–69, 218
college culture 9, 11, 16, 30, 39–41, 44, 75, 101, 116–117, 124, 139, 166, 173, 195, 200
college foundation 5, 85, 111–119, 158, 192–193, 216

COMBASE 207
communications 24–25, 56, 58, 66, 69, 77, 106, 161
Community College Baccalaureate Association (CCBA) 209
Community College Business Officers 212
Community College Research Center at Columbia University (CCRC) 214
Community Colleges for International Development (CCID) 209
Community Colleges Humanities Association (CCHA) 210
Community Colleges of Appalachia (CCA) 207
Council for Advancement and Support of Education (CASE) 211
Council for Resource Development (CRD) 212
COVID-19 pandemic 6, 175–176
Creamer, Mary Elizabeth 132, 224
Creery, Mark 2, 3, 223
Cuthbertson, James 63, 182, 224

danger zone 7, 93, 160–161, 162
Darwin, Charles 177
day one 12
decision-making 168–169
development officer 111–112
digital and social media 107–108
diversity 45, 48, 138, 150, 216
donor cultivation 41, 86, 93, 111–116
Dubois, Glenn 14, 39, 63, 191–192, 224
Dunnavant, Siobhan 224

economic development 29, 117, 127–135, 215
ego management 13, 136–137, 142
elevator speech 13, 15
enrollment 46, 97, 110, 122, 124, 130, 150, 167, 184–185, 201, 211, 215, 220

227

Index

entertainment 115–116, 129, 146–147
ethics 9, 21, 139
evaluation 22, 31, 57–58, 82–83, 148–155, 159
executive assistant 13, 145, 147
Executive Leadership Institute (ELI) 193–194
external 16, 23, 42–44, 63, 113–117

failure 14, 142, 176, 217
faith-based communities 91, 103–106
Farrell, Patrick 94, 224
financial pressures 46, 137, 167, 177
first impressions 10–13, 19, 199
foundation board 5, 111–113, 158, 161, 192–193
Frost, David 14
fundraising 109–119, 150, 192–194, 205, 211, 216, 221
Future Presidents Institute (FPI) 194

government relations 120–126, 172, 217, 221
Groover, Richard 224

Hamel, Dana B. 3, 224
helicopter parents 169–170
helpful tip 7, 9, 22, 23–24, 29, 35, 37, 43–44, 53, 59–60, 113, 125, 130, 145, 149, 154, 159, 163–164, 192–193, 195
hiring and firing 20, 22, 47, 57–58, 61, 139–140, 148–159

Instructional Technology Council 210
internal 16, 22–23, 42–43, 58, 67, 71–72, 194, 113–117
interviews 9, 11–12, 14, 139–141, 153–154, 188, 196–205, 215

Kaine, Tim 1–2, 224
key chapter takeaways 7, 19, 27, 33, 50, 58, 77, 89–90, 108, 119, 126, 135, 142, 147, 159, 164, 187, 205
Kraus, Jeffrey 138, 224

lame duck president 162
Lane, James 121, 224
leadership 5–6, 8, 35–36, 39, 42–43, 50, 67, 69, 71, 93–94, 125, 141–142, 152, 171, 181, 215–216, 222
League for Innovation in the Community College 193–194, 208

leveraging 44, 91–92
Loope, David 15, 224

Madère, Whit 71, 225
Manzari, John 20, 141, 225
Martin, John 177, 225
McDade, Sharon 45, 202, 225
meeting dynamics 48–49
mentoring 15, 206, 210, 212
mission 5, 11, 15, 17, 21–22, 27–30, 32–33, 55, 84, 86–88, 92, 99, 118–119, 139, 183, 200
Moret, Stephen 134–135, 225

National Alliance of Concurrent Enrollment Partnerships (NACEP) 211
National Association of Community College Entrepreneurship (NACCE) 208
National Association of Community College Teacher Education Programs (NACCTEP) 211
National Association of State Directors of Community Colleges (NASDCC) 214
National Association of Student Personnel Administrators (NASPA) 209
National Council for Continuing Education and Training 213
National Institute for Staff and Organizational Development (NISOD) 213
Nixon, Richard 14
non-profits 102–103, 166–167

partnerships 1, 64, 77, 83, 91–92, 94–108
personal visibility 10, 19
politics 13, 18–19, 29, 40, 63–64, 120–126, 138–139, 181–182
presidential search 22, 157, 162–164, 190, 193–202
presidential search questions 215–222
president's spouse 37, 98, 146–147
press and media 107, 187

Rainone, John 117, 225
Rao, Michael 100, 225
Raspiller, Theodore 93, 133, 225
relationships 11, 13, 41–44, 68–69, 77, 91–99, 108, 110–111, 113, 116–118, 120–123, 150, 162, 168, 182
resumé 194–196, 205
Rhodes, Gary 2–3, 9, 34, 223
Rhodes, Nam 146, 179–180, 225
Roberson, Stewart 98, 225

Index

Scheeler, Kim 95, 225
Serenity Prayer 59, 77, 125
sexual harassment 141
shared governance 46, 51, 67–68
Sherman, Vaughn 20, 225
stackable credentials 133–134
stakeholders 10, 12, 29, 92–93
Steiner, Edward 3–4, 225
Sullivan, Monty 66, 182, 226
system office 29, 51, 53, 58, 65–66, 70–71, 157, 171, 175

team building 44–48, 74–77, 138
technology 88, 174–177, 196, 221
thank-yous 10, 17, 200
threats 165–187

Trani, Eugene 226
trust 16, 66, 69, 113, 118, 217

unfunded mandates 70, 165
universal truth 7, 13, 34, 53, 58, 154, 155, 165, 166, 179

values 11, 13, 20, 29, 30, 33, 36, 39–50, 68, 72–73, 137, 142

Wheelan, Belle S. 31–32, 226
work-life balance 15, 37, 143–144
workforce development 13, 62, 98, 107, 127–135, 158
World Future Society (WFS) 214

www.ingramcontent.com/pod-product-compliance
Lightning Source LLC
Chambersburg PA
CBHW032039300426
44117CB00009B/1122